Our Forgotten Years

A Gypsy woman's life on the road

Our Forgotten Years

A Gypsy woman's life on the road

Maggie Smith-Bendell

University of Hertfordshire Press

First published in Great Britain in 2009 by
University of Hertfordshire Press
College Lane
Hatfield
Hertfordshire AL10 9AB

British Library Cataloguing in Publication Data
A catalogue record for this book is available from the British Library

ISBN 978-1-902806-91-4

Design by Mathew Lyons
Printed in Great Britain by CPI Antony Rowe, Chippenham, SN14 6LH

Front cover:
The Mendips, Somerset, c.1936. See page 211.
The author on the steps of one of her vardos © Cherry Coles.

Back cover:
The author with Lord Avebury, 2009 © Sally Woodbury-Tucker.
Pea-picking, North Petherton, c.1940s. See page 53.

Contents

Chapter One

My Family

I AM A ROMANI GYPSY GAL. I was born on the edge of a pea field at Thurloxton, near Bridgwater in Somerset, on the 15th of July 1941. I was given the name Margaret which changed, over the years, to Maggie. I also had a nickname – as many Travellers do – which was 'Two Foot', though I have never found out why.

My family are descended from a group of people who first came to this country many centuries ago. We live by the old customs of our traditional way of life. We travel up and down the countryside, earning our living from the hedgerows, catching rabbits, pheasants and wild duck. We use elder and hazel from the hedges to make clothes pegs and beautiful wooden flowers, which we sell round the house-dwellers' doors. We also do all manner of fieldwork for farmers: picking peas, beans and hops, cutting and topping swedes, picking up tatters, and many other kinds of work. Our men are masters at stone-walling and hedge-laying. Our kind of work has been handed down through the generations, from father to son, mother to daughter, and will continue so.

Me dad was a wonderful, wise man. He was called Lenard Smith and was born and bred in the lanes of Somerset. He really was a wise old bird, and could always find ways to earn his living, or at least make ends meet. He was one of twelve children, nine boys and three gals. The boys' names were Tom, Jessie, Joe, John, Lenard, Jim, Dan, Alfie and Little Ikie. The gals were Jane (known as 'Touwie'), Emily and Little Alice. Me granny was Emma Smith-Orchard from Hampshire, and granddad was Dannal Butler from Somerset and Wiltshire.

When Little Alice was about four years old, her frock caught aflame from the outside fires that we use daily and she died from her burns. Ikie never did stand much of a chance: as a very small infant me granny took him into her bed, and one night in her sleep she rolled over on top of him and squashed poor little Ikie stone dead. They say he was as flat as a pancake the next morning.

Me mam was Defiance Small, better known as 'Little Fiance' or 'Vie'. Her family came from Devonshire and she was born in Plymouth but lived most of her young life in and around Newton Abbot. Me granddad's name was Old Jim Small. All his family was Devonshire born and bred for many generations. Me real granny was Minnie Black, who came from Hampshire, though sadly we never knew her for she died aged twenty-six, when her children were very young, leaving me granddad Jim with six little children to bring up. Again, two of them children – Leonard and Vashtie – died as infants. That left Bobby, Ellen, Jeannie and me mam, Defiance.

Granddad took another wife, Annie, who came from the old family of Ayres from Bristol, and went on to have a second family of children. In all, they reckon me granddad Jim fathered twenty-one children.

It was hard going, back in those early days. The death rate in young children was very high indeed and we needlessly lost many of our people because of lack of medical help. But me mam was to know tragic times all through her life, as you shall see from my story.

Runaways: mam and dad in c.1936 when they 'ran away' to Bridgwater and got married. Dad was long and thin like a peg stick, mam was as pretty as paint.

Me mam and dad met in the pea fields at Bridgwater in Somerset. At this time we knew each other as Travellers, so I will refer to ourselves this way. There were many Travelling families out working in the hot, sunny pea fields, families from all parts of the country – Wiltshire, Oxford, Devon, Cornwall, Gloucester – they would all meet and work for the Coles, the Wigleys and other various pea-growers. Our family usually picked for old Jim Cole or McWilliams.

Me mam was only sixteen when she ran away with me dad in the year of 1935 (or thereabouts). He was a few years older than she, but they stayed together till their eighties when death parted them. They had eight children and I was the second eldest. Alfie was born at Torbay in Devonshire; Robert was born on the Novers, Bedminster, Bristol; Little Jessie and Emily were born at Devizes, Wiltshire; Holly was born at Drumbridges in Devonshire, and Richard and Maralyn were both born in Bath.

Our family was small compared to most families of that time – many families had ten, twelve or even more children – but me dad said we elder four were his little army of workers. My family was and is a close, loving one. We had a good mam and dad who never were shy at putting their shoulder to the wheel when it came to work.

Working was the main stay of our life. We had to work or starve. In the summer we would be out on the pea and broad-bean fields from four am until tea-time, come rain or wind or shine. In winter the men would be out at peep of daylight, frozen stiff, topping swedes, sometimes cutting off fingers with the sharp knives without even knowing it. That's how cold them winters were back then. There was also the back-breaking work of following the farmer on his tractor, picking up tatters. Come autumn it would be picking apples and plums, and then on to the hop gardens. Not forgetting the hay-making season. It was work, and the Travellers were glad of it.

Chapter Two

A Fearful Winter

M Y EARLY THOUGHTS TAKE ME BACK to that memorable journey as we came back from the hop gardens of Ledbury, back down to Wiltshire. It would be a long, hard travel; we were heading for a little common at Melksham, where me dad knew he and his brother Jim would have winter work on a farm known to them. They would be hedge-laying and cutting up logs on an old saw bench. We had arranged to spend winter together with Jim, May and their three children, but they had not come hop-picking this year so we had to meet them on the road on our way back.

"I can smell snow in the air," said me dad.

"Lenard, that nose of yours will get you in trouble one of these days," me mam replied. "If me mind serves me right, there's a nice bake-house in the next village. It must be getting near dinner time, so pull over when we reaches it, and I'll do a bit of shopping."

"Right Vie, and I'll give me horses a rest."

Although it was cold outside, our wagon was as warm as toast, for in all wagons was a little Queenie stove made of ornate iron, standing on its own three pretty legs. They would burn coal or wood, and we could boil a kettle or keep a stew hot as we travelled along. Alfie, Robert and I felt a bit sad as we left the hop gardens, for we had made many good friends, as had me mam and dad. We had to say farewell to old family and friends that we met each year; like us they would be travelling dozens of different roads back to their part of the country, probably thinking the same thoughts as we did. Autumn was a kushtie[1] season and full of good company.

As the village came into sight, me dad dropped me and me mam off to do the shopping and went to pull in just outside the village and light a fire. It was near the end of November and would soon be Christmas, and we'd been promised a good one this year for sticking by the hop crib and picking alongside me mam and dad. Me dad used to say it was one man's work to keep we three at it, as we loved to wander off fetching wood or playing with the other Traveller children. If I was threatened once to stand and pick, it must have been a thousand times: "Maggie my gal, stand and pick a few hops for your old dad, or I'll give you a hiding!" But he'd never beat us – it was me mam who'd put one across us if we didn't watch out.

The village shop was on the verge of closing for dinner, so we just made it. Two loaves, a sticky lardy cake and a few pounds of tatters saw us walking out the village and back towards the wagon, and the welcome sight of a big red-hot fire. As we drew near I saw our six banty hens, which we kept for eggs, stretching their legs by the wagon. They were kept boxed on the tail rack at night and while we travelled. We also kept two horses – Patchie, who was a piebald, black and white, and Ticker who was a skewbald, brown and white – and two Jack Russell dogs for rabbiting.

The hop-picking had lasted a bit longer that year and so we were late meeting up with Jim.

---

1. good; fine

"I'll travel a few more miles each day to make the time up," dad told me mam. "At least our horses are fresh from weeks of doing next to nothing."

"Well you should have said afore I went to the shop. We ain't got many candles, and the wagon lamps take up two at a time."

"Never mind," answered me dad. "There's another village further on, we'll get a few there; it won't get dark till around four o'clock."

As we sat round the fire eating fried bacon and tatters, dipping our new bread in the fat and enjoying a rest, who did we see coming at us in the distance but the village policeman.

"Now Lenard, afore he gets here, don't back-chat him," warned me mam. "You knows he'll lock you up."

"My Vie, I gets sick to me teeth with they men. We ain't been here an hour and they's on us already."

"Just mind what happened afore, when they took you for cheeking them back. Me and my children was stuck in the road for days on our own."

"All right, Vie, I'll keep me gab shut."

We three knew better than to speak in front of the policeman, but me mam always had to warn me dad. It was very rare that we'd get a civil one coming up to us, and this one was no different. Up he came with his pushbike, right up to the fire.

"You can't stop here," said the policeman. "Put that fire out and get moving."

"We have only just stopped to feed our children, sir," me mam explained.

"I don't care what made you stop, now get moving."

"Hang on," said me dad. "My woman told you why we stopped. Ain't we allowed to eat like everyone else then?"

"Not on my patch," he snarled at my dad. "Now get on your way."

"Let me tell you something, mister. This patch – your patch – will be here long after you're dead and gone," said me dad.

"I don't want any threats from you," answered the policeman, "or I'll run you in."

"Len, Len," whispered my mam. "Hush for gawd's sake, my Len."

"Well, who do he think he is?" my dad replied.

The policeman stayed right there until we'd harnessed the horses and put out the fire. He was still watching us as we travelled on down the road.

"One of these days, my Vie, I'm going to stretch one of they policemen out like a mackerel. They just don't give up!"

"And that day, Len, you'll get yourself six months' hard labour."

"I know, Vie, but they makes me blood boil, they do. It don't cost nothing to be civil, now do it?"

"In a few more days we'll be tucked up on the farm," she told him.

"Any road," said me dad, "I'm going to pull over. We need some short bits of wood for the stove; I never got time back there to fetch any."

We pulled in on the grass verge and gathered an armful of wood each to keep the wagon warm as we still had a long way to go afore me dad would pull up for the night. It wasn't good to travel the roads in the dark, but needs must. At least we had lights to let other road users know we were travelling.

We lived a slow way of life, at the pace of our horses. In the winter we three children found the travelling hard. When the spring and summer came we could run in front or behind the wagon, but winter was too cold for that. I never liked being penned in, and it set me and our Alfie fighting. We were always fighting, or so me mam said.

"When we pulls in for the night and I've washed you two, it's bed for you both. No supper for you two," threatened me mam.

"We ain't dirty," said our Robert.

"We'll see who's dirty when we stops," said me mam.

How I hated me mam washing me! That carbolic soap got up your nose and into your eyes, and didn't it smart! We always ended up crying after a wash. I thought she took delight in it, for she washed us several times a day.

We kept going for a few more days, until we finally met up with Jim and May and their two sons, Jimmy and baby Checkers, and daughter Lilea. It was good to have company again as we made our way to Melksham Common. We would stop there a few days afore we went onto the farm.

There were a lot of wagons pulled up on the common, and we knew all of the families in them. It was fun running with the other children, dressed up against the cold to fetch wood and water. All the families that were pulled up on the common were still hoping to find winter work, so me dad thought how lucky he was to have a work place already lined up to go on to. Had he known what it would lead to he would not have been so pleased with himself. Fear itself was waiting for my family on that farm.

Over the years I have thought long and hard about what happened after we pulled up on the farm. How uneducated we were; how unworldly my people. We must have been in a world of our own. A question put to our parents by the farmer sent them mad for weeks, and it broke our hearts to see our family so full of fright.

We had worked on the farm before and pulled up as usual. It was important to find work with a farmer in the winter months, for that was the only way we could get a supply of hay for the horses in the long, cold months ahead. We knew this farmer quite well, but not so his woman. She always kept to herself but he knew our names and would often have a joke with us.

Me dad and Uncle Jim had been working laying the hedges for a week. It had snowed heavily, which we children thought was grand, and were having a fine old time, getting excited because it was nearly Christmas. A few more days and we could hang our socks up! Not that we looked for dolly prams or bikes; we knew we would not get anything big, simply because we had nowhere to carry it. Our wagon was packed to the hilt as it was, but it was so exciting anyway.

One afternoon, the farmer's wife came to the little paddock that we had pulled up on, bringing eggs for us children. The next morning she came again, bringing mince pies and telling me mam how good and well behaved we children were. When she left, me mam turned to May. "What's up with her, then? She don't bother with the likes of we lot."

"I was thinking the same, my Vie," answered May, growing suspicious.

"May, that woman is up to no good, but we can't say nothing to her. Our men needs the work."

They agreed to keep quiet and tried to think little of it. The woman usually kept to herself, but back she came that same afternoon. I could see me mam was not happy.

"What can I do for you, lady?" Me mam had a gleam in her eyes. "We don't normally see you when we stops here."

"Oh, I just like to see your children, and I shall have a little something for them on Christmas morning."

"Don't put yourself out for my lot," said me mam, though we were more than a little interested at the thought of extra presents. "They got plenty already. Thank you all the same," she added, and the woman left. "Alfie, an' you Maggie, take this hot bottle of tea an' bread an' cheese over the fields to your dad."

This we loved to do, for we could play snowballs without getting told off. Jimmy and Lilea came too with bottles for their dad. We were full of ourselves, imagining what sweet gifts the farmer's wife might give to us on Christmas day.

Me dad was pleased to get a hot drink, even though they had a big roaring fire going to burn up the bracken. We stopped and had a warm-up before making our way back to the paddock.

"You lot!" shouted me dad after us. "Pick up a armful of wood each and take it back to the wagon."

"We knows that," we hollered back, loading ourselves up like pack-horses for the long struggle back across the two fields. We always needed firewood for the stove and fire.

We met the farmer halfway back, who laughed kindly when he saw us crossing the field. "What a big load of wood you all got." That too was strange, for the farmer rarely went over to me dad and Jim. He didn't have to, for he always knew that they worked well.

"He's checking on me dad," said our Alfie.

"Well, he won't catch they two playing snowballs," I said, and thought no more of it. We got back to the wagons and threw down the wood near the fire that we shared with Jim and May.

"Now go and fetch a can of water, so I can cook a nice hot meal for when your dad gets back," we were told. That meant going into the farmyard to the tap, which we had done many times before, but this time we noticed the farmer's wife watching us from her doorway. She never spoke, but kept her eyes on us as we went. As we got back with the can, up came Jim and me dad, though they weren't due back for hours yet. Me dad looked white and shaky.

Me mam approached him. "What's up, my Len, have the man sacked you?"

"No, my Vie, it's much worse than that. Start packing the things up, we gotta shift out of here."

"But we can't shift! We got snow up to our eyeballs and the night's coming in. Is you mad? What have you done, eh?"

"I ain't done nothing, it's that man. He wants to take my Alfie off us."

"What?" Mam was strangely quiet. "What did you just say?"

"It's true," said Jim. "He come out to us and asked if he could have your Alfie to keep. To bring him up."

"What?" said me mam. "Pack up quick! And you, Alfie, get up in that wagon and stay there!"

The men were running to fetch the horses. Everything had turned upside down. We were running around like headless chickens, throwing things up in the wagon and on to the tail rack. Our world had suddenly gone mad.

Me dad and Jim were cutting up sack-bags to tie on the horses' hoofs, to stop them slipping in the hard-packed snow out on the road.

When they pulled the wagons they would tend to slip on the glassy road and not be able to get a grip. Just as we were about to pull out, the farmer and his woman came to the gate, both pleading for us to think about what we were about to do.

"I will look after him," the woman was trying to tell me mam.

"Go and get your own children! You ain't having mine!" Me mam bore down on the farmer's wife until me dad grabbed hold of her and shoved her up into the wagon.

"Stay there, Vie! Stay put!"

"I'll swing for that woman, Lenard!"

Full of fear that they would take our Alfie, we pulled out onto the dangerous road, leaving the washing still hung on the hedge, the six little banties, and a lot of other things we could not afford to lose.

But we had each other. We were still a complete family.

It was a night that would haunt us for months to come. Any minute we expected the police to pull us up and take our Alfie from us. Although travelling in the snow, especially in the dark, was unheard of for Travellers, we knew we had to get away from that area.

The world was white, so it wasn't too dark that night, but it was very dangerous for the horses to travel in the snow. One slip and they could break a leg; if the wagon began to slide it could drag the horses with it and roll on top of the men. They had made thick horseshoes out of the old sack-bags to help the horses grip, but this would not save them in a fall.

It was a nightmare. We had never been in such a predicament before. We had not gone far when me dad pulled up to talk to his brother Jim. They had not said where we could make for before we had pulled out.

"The best place to head for," said Jim, "is on Chapel Plaister. There'll be lots of other Travellers pulled up and we can get lost amongst them."

"Which is the best road to take, then?" asked me dad, for we could not afford to take a hilly road, it would be far too dangerous.

I don't know the exact mileage from Melksham to Chapel Plaister Common, but it could be five miles by the back roads. We were travelling so slow it took hours. Thank god we had packed wood for the stove so at least we could keep warm. Not so for the grown-ups, for the two men were walking and sliding at their horses' heads, trying to coax them on and hold them up as they went. Me mam was standing on the foreboard, ready to jump off and help me dad if it came to it. The heavy wagons could cause problems. It wouldn't take much for them to slide all over the road, so it was sheer guts and determination that kept them going.

All this time our poor Alfie was frit[2] to death. He and we others never understood what was really going on but we knew that whatever it took, me mam and dad would protect us from any danger. We had a deep trust in them.

We travelled at not even a horse's regular pace, creeping along. I remember the moon coming out to guide us, and our world had a blue tinge to it. As we crept past country cottages we could see and smell the coal-smoke from their fires, and they never knew we were passing them by. Once an old fox pelted across our path, but neither our Patchie nor Ticker blinked an eyelid.

The hours felt like days to us, and even though me mam told us to get to sleep we could not, for we felt their worries and heard them muttering to each other. In and out, me dad and Jim would call to each other, asking if all was well. I believe it was only because of the surefootedness of our horses that we finally pulled on to Chapel Plaister, tired and worried but finally safe.

The Travellers on the common had all bedded down for the night and got a fright when the dogs started to bark at us. Heads poked out of their wagons as we pulled up.

---

2. frightened

"What's up?" they called. "Who is it out there?"

"It's me, Lenard," answered me dad. "We got trouble on our hands."

At that statement, men and women climbed down out of their warm wagons and into the cold, snowy air.

"What's wrong, Lenard? Hang on, I'll make the fire up, you lot looks scrammed[3]!"

"They tried to take me boy off me." It was all me dad could get out, so very cold was he.

"Who did?" someone asked.

"The farmer mush," cried me mam.

Some of the men took over our wagons, unhitching the horses and pulling the wagons right close to theirs.

"Fetch a bundle of that hay off me tail-rack," called one man. "Come on, you boys, jump to it!"

Everyone was jittery by now: a child was under threat, that's all they knew for sure.

After hot cups of sweet tea were made and we were warming by the big fire, me dad told all what had happened. At last, we had our people to protect us, no one would get anywhere near our Alfie now, and oh, that felt kushtie!

"Well," said one big-bodied young man. "Let them come here and try and take any child. They'll go faster than they come, I can tell you."

It was months after we ran away from that farm that me mam found out, from the house-dwellers we sold wild flowers to, that a farmer had no right to just take our children.

When asked if they could, one housewife was astounded and said, "That's not true, my dear. No one can just take a child from its family."

Not satisfied, me mam and May asked the same question to many of

---

3. frozen

the house-dwellers, who all told them the same thing.

"So it must be true then, May," me mam said.

"It must be, my Vie, and just look what they put us through that night. We could have all been killed stone dead, an' our horses with us."

Thinking back on all this, it must have been hell for my people back in them years. To think that if any gorgie[4] wanted one of our children they could just take them. How they must have lived in fear! I know me mam and dad did, for we always gave that farm a wide berth after that. We knew only that laws counted against us, that we were always in the wrong. It must have been a living nightmare.

There is an old saying that ignorance is bliss. In this case it wasn't bliss at all. The Travellers of those days were very wise and skilled in many ways but never knew a thing about education or the law. They must have been like children to the police, who bullied and harassed them on a daily basis. The police would put them in jail for answering back. What a fearful life they must have led, and not just in them days, but for hundreds of generations before that.

Many kings and queens have created laws to restrict the movement and rights of British Gypsies, some ordering imprisonment, emigration, or even execution for our lifestyle. King Edward VI passed a law that ordered Gypsies to be branded and enslaved. What a nice man he must've been! The last known execution for the crime of 'being a Gypsy' in England was under Oliver Cromwell, but even now our nomadic lifestyle is still considered a criminal one.

---

4. A non-Romani, a house-dweller; usually pronounced 'gor-ja' in Anglo-Romani dialects. Also written 'gadjé'.

Chapter Three

The War Years

THAT NIGHT, WE SAT AROUND OUR FIRE as me mam and May explained what the house-dwellers had told them in the day. We children felt safe like we never had, knowing that no gorgie could take us away from our family. It was that night, if me memory serves me right, that I first learned of how the Travellers served our country during the World Wars.

Me mam was cooking over the fire, assuring us of Alfie's safety.

"Well, what were we to think?" me dad said. "Look how they treated us in the war, back then."

"Yeah," said Jim. "They took the lot of us, with no bye nor leave."

"You know, my Len," said May, "I still thinks about they horses they took off us, and wonder if any of them ever came home again."

"Don't know, May, an' we never will know. Poor bloody animals, they must have got shell-shocked if not killed outright."

"I shan't ever forget," said me mam.

"Nor will any other Traveller," Jim promised.

It had been hard on all of us, me mam explained. The men and horses had been taken without explanation, and for weeks she didn't know if Lenard had been dead or alive. She'd been left in the lonely lanes near Wedmore, with no grys[5] to shift the wagon. She had been lucky if the shops had been able to sell her a bit of flour and fat to make puddings or pancakes with. This was in the early years of the War, not long after me man and dad got together.

Me mam told us how she had been cooking a bit of dinner, when from up the road came two army lorries, full of soldiers. They thought the lorries would pass them by, but up they pulled and several soldiers got out holding guns. For a brief moment, Little Fiance had thought they were Germans and would shoot the whole family there an' then, but then they spoke up in English. They asked how many men and boys the family had, and poor old Henry, who had been travelling with my parents at the time, asked them why they wanted to know.

"We're here to take your men for the army," one of the soldiers replied.

One of them made a grab for me dad, but he was too quick for them, jumping over the moor ditch to run across the fields. Well, it had been bedlam. Some of the soldiers jumped the ditches and took off after him to bring him back.

They took Lenard and one of Old Henry's boys off in the lorries, leaving the family with no men to fend for them except for the very old and children. Not knowing what to do, Henry suggested they stay put.

"We'll see what comes of it all," he told me mam. "At least our lot will know where to find us, if they are let loose."

Fearful of the bombing, they decided they had to pull off the main roads and avoid the big towns, so shifted up the lanes and pulled into Dead Mary's Lane. From there, me mam planned to walk to Cheddar and Axbridge to go calling[6] and get shopping, but the next day the army lorries returned to them.

---

5. horses

6. Calling at the houses in villages and towns was a way to hawk (sell) flowers and other
   crafts to gorgies, or exchange for old clothes or scrap wood and metal.

"We ain't got no more men for you to take," said one or t'other, but the soldiers approached the same as they had before.

"We haven't come for the men," said one. "We want your horses."

Old Henry and Little Fiance were distraught as the soldiers took all the horses off the plug chains and took their harnesses as well! They were left with two young, unbroken colts and no harnesses with which to break them in. The soldiers let down a ramp on the back of a lorry and that was the last they ever saw of the grys.

It was only a few weeks later that Lenard returned for the first time. He'd been put on fire-watch in Bristol, but had been so worried about his Vie and the children that he escaped back to us. The army soon caught up with him and took him back, but that wouldn't stop me dad. For months this went on: he would escape and return to the family and the army would pick him up and take him back again.

Eventually, Lenard's brother, Jessie, found me mam in the lanes. Neither he nor his horse had been taken with the other men, for he was a cripple and his old horse was skin and bones, but he was able to slowly shift the wagons in relay, taking each a few miles before returning for the next. To earn money for food, the women learned men's work and spent their days cutting the swedes and picking tatters to earn a few shillings in and out.

All the while, Lenard had been running from the army to find his family. Each time he tried to escape he was caught again, before he'd had time to do more than catch a few shushies[7].

"But I got back to you, didn't I, my Vie?" I remember me dad saying. "I couldn't rest, not knowing if a bomb had dropped on you and killed all I had left."

"You did," me mam agreed, "and many more Traveller men did the same. We was all in the same boat."

---

7. rabbits

Hearing my family talk about the war years, I never could understand why I had so little memory of our struggles. Their words stayed in my memory for years.

We Travellers felt like a people without a country of our own, being told each day that we didn't belong, that we had to move on, that our sort weren't wanted here or there – and yet they were forced to fight as British people.

My parents told many tales about their narrow escapes. In one, me dad had just got back to the wagon after running from the army for the last time. They thought that if they travelled on their own and hid in the lanes they could be together, and so got an old pony which could just about pull the wagon and went to where me granddad Dannal was born, which we called 'Dannal's Basin'. It was close to Chilcompton, near Midsomer Norton. They went to pull into a nearby gateway, but me dad had a bad feeling about the area and refused to stop there. They continued on down the lane, not too far, and sure enough during the night that gateway was bombed, a large crater was all that was left of that farmer's field.

I can remember old Henry telling us about the Great War, and a rhyme his own mother made up about the violence:

I never borned my son
To carry a gun,
Or shoot and kill
A mother's son.

Many of us felt that way. We Travellers were not born to kill people but many of our men had to, because they were forced to fight and kill over the seas. Many mothers' sons and husbands never came back. They fought alongside the gorgies and got killed and very little is said of that, and while the towns and villages had Home Guards to look after them, we poor Travellers had nobody to care if we lived or starved to death.

The countryside was very messed up after the war, and Lenard and the others would get jobs clearing up – burning rubbish and collecting old twisted iron to sell to the scrapyards. We were some of the lucky ones, they told us. Many Traveller men and boys sent overseas – to fight or work with the horses – never came back, and still lay thousands of miles from home. But never forgotten.

Round the fire, we sat spellbound as we listened to me parents talking of their sad experience during those old times.

"I had to buy an old miler[8] to pull an old trap, so we could go and fetch grub for the children to eat," said me dad. "But we made it in the end, my Vie, didn't we?"

"Yes, my Len, we made it, but only by the skin of our teeth. I hope to God we never lives to see another war."

---

8. donkey

Chapter Four

Snowdrop Woods

SOON IT WAS TIME TO LEAVE our friends from off the common. Christmas had hardly been a Christmas for us, but me mam promised to make up for it next year. It was time to travel to the wild snowdrops, and get back to earning a few shillings, so with May and Jim we set off for the copses where we knew we could pick them in peace. It wasn't against the law in that day and age to pick wild flowers, so we knew it would cause no trouble for us.

"It's a different journey from the last one we made," said Jim to me dad, thinking of the escape from the farm at Melksham.

"I shan't forget the last one in a hurry," me dad agreed. "Get yourself off, Jim. Today I will follow your tracks, eh?"

We said our thanks and farewells to the lovely families that had taken such good care of us that dreadful night and set out for new pastures. As me dad always liked to be one of the first to get to the copses, we had left early, hoping to pull up and pick what we needed and then be off to sell them before anyone else. It didn't always work out this way, but he gave it a good try each year.

It was good to be back on the road, travelling through village after village, stopping here and there. Sometimes we met other wagons going the opposite way, or caught up to wagons ahead on the road and spent a few hours with them before setting off again. We knew every Traveller on these roads – or thought we did, at least.

February was a cold old month with lots of hard frost and sometimes the snow would come down, but that year there were only the early morning frosts, which we could put up with. A good, big fire would put the frost in its place wherever we pulled in. We'd not earned any money for weeks, so things were getting tight in our pockets. Our Patchie and Ticker ate the new young grass-shoots as they had not had their feeds of hay so much as other years. It was a bad time all round.

We depended on the horses for our very lives and livelihoods – we could not get our living without them – and so Traveller horses were put before all else. They were often looked after better than us, specially bred to pull our wagons, carts and trolleys. Their colour is special, too: we love our piebalds – jet black and white – and skewbalds – red or dark brown and white. There are also red roans, blue roans, shiny dark bays, greys and the all-black. It's the piebalds and skewbalds that are the favourites, but all are loved and cared for.

At last we reached the Snowdrop Woods, me dad and Jim with smiles on their faces. Yes, we were the first Travellers to get there, and so the copse was all ours. We could pick in peace to our hearts' delight.

As the evening was drawing in, me dad said we could pick our first basketful while he and Jim set up a tidy fire for when we got back, and the old kettle would be singing on the kettle iron. Dressed warm in jackets and wellies, I set off with our Alfie and Robert while Little Jess stayed with me dad. Our baby sister Emily was left snug in the wagon. May also went into the woods with Jimmy and Lilea to help us collect more. No matter who picked what, all the flowers would be bunched and shared between the two families at the end of the day. It was custom, I supposed: we always shared anything that might earn us a living – be it flowers, pegs or whatever – with the folk we travelled with.

It was cold in the copse and the white clumps of snowdrops stood out waiting to be picked. Their white heads, tinged with green near the stem, were beautiful to behold. They grouped together, it seemed, to protect each other from the sight of humans. Maybe it was fancy, but that's how I saw them as the light faded – like blobs of snow left over from winter. They would end up in some house-dweller's warm kitchen, on a table or window ledge, hanging their heads down shyly as though not to be seen.

"Maggie, get picking," said me mam. "You're here to pick, not to admire. That won't fill your belly."

"She ain't got no sense, she ain't no good at picking," said our Alfie, that little mush.

"Shut your gab! I can pick better and faster than you."

Our Robert perked up at that. "You can't out-pick me!"

"Who woke you up?" I asked him.

"Maggie, I shan't warn you no more. Now pick on, there's a good gal," called me mam.

So I started to pick, and me mind wandered. "Mam, ain't it a shame to pick these little flowers? They'll only die in they houses."

"I'll 'die' you if you don't get on with it," she hollered at me. "Now shut up and pick."

I did as told, moving closer to our Alfie as I picked at each clump.

"Go and pick your own flowers, these is mine round here."

"I'm trying to keep out of the brambles, ain't I?" It seemed the best of the flowers grew in the brambles.

"Go away, our Maggie, or I'll hit you one."

"You go away, afore I hits you," I told him.

With that, our Alfie pushed me straight into the bramble bush! I never saw it coming and screamed like a loony as I was scratched to pieces by the thorns in me legs and bum.

"I'll kill you now!" I hollered at him, cold and crying and mad as hell, and off he ran! Alfie knew better than to stand his ground when me temper was up.

"Right, you two, that's a hiding for you," shouted me mam.

Lilea was laughing at me, so I snoped[9] her, as our Alfie was out of me reach.

"Hark, hark," said May suddenly, stopping our fights immediately. "Somebody's a-coming."

"It could be one of they old tramps," me mam replied.

"Better get ourselves a good stick each," said May. "You never knows what they old men will do."

Soon we could all hear someone treading heavily through the trees. That shut me up quick! I was frit to death of old tramps and picked up a stick to beat this one with, in case he got cheeky to me mam.

May began to laugh as a man came out of the dense woods, and soon we could recognise me dad's older brother, Joe – Cock-eye Joe as he was known – coming towards us.

"It's only you, Joe!" exclaimed May.

"What's you laughing at?" he asked her.

"She thought you was one of they old tramps coming at us," answered me mam.

"Well, I ain't no tramp," he cried.

"We knows that now," soothed May, "but put yourself in our place! Here we is, deep in the copse nearly on dark, and we hears some man a-coming – what would you have thought, eh?"

"We just pulled in with your lot," Joe explained, "an' I thought as how I'd start picking a few flowers for my Allie. Give her a start for tomorrow."

We all apologised to him, and explained how he'd put the frits on us all. The fear and relief had taken me mind off me own problems for a

9. hit

minute or two, but now I could see the blood from the bramble thorns running all down me legs. I turned to me mam with a grimace.

"That's it, mam. I shan't pick no more the day. I'm off back to me dad."

"If you don't pick a few more, you won't come out a-calling with me," she threatened.

"Well, I will tell me dad on the lot of you when I do get back," I said, but carried on picking under her direction. Soon our Robert began to cry out that he was too cold to pick, and Alfie too was trembling with the cold.

"That's it," said me mam, seeing how chilled we were and frit that we should catch our deaths. "Let's pick our way back. We ain't done too bad, as a start."

Oh, it was good to get back to the fire, where we were soon treated to a fry-up: eggs, bacon and fried bread. Me mam would buy half a side of home-cured bacon whenever she could get it, and so our slices were thick and tasty.

After we had eaten, we gathered round the fire and began to bunch up our pickings in the light it gave off. We had stopped at an old cottage on our way to the woods, begging an armful of box – a small-leafed evergreen with a good, strong smell to it – to use as a backing to the snowdrops and little wild daffies that we would bunch together. We broke the box down to fit the size of the snowdrops, using it as backing as we made up our bunches, tying them off with strings of unravelled wool from an old gansey[10]. We placed our finished bunches in a small tin bath of water to keep them fresh for the two or three days we would spend picking. As long as they were kept cold, the flowers would last for ages, long after we'd set out on the road, seeking villages in which to sell them.

The following morning, me dad gave our Alfie a dire warning to leave me alone while we were in the copses. "You leave my Maggie be,"

---

10. A thick knitted jumper, originally designed for fishermen.

I heard him say to my brother, "She's a good girl!" Of course, that was a load of old flannel – I knew he'd only said it so that I'd go out and pick with the rest of them. Me dad thought I didn't know what he was up to, but I did. I weren't daft!

That morning, Allie came out with us, as well as her Joe, but their girl Cathy had to stay round the fire for she was nearly blind. But oh, she was a case! She was twelve years old and could sing 'The Laughing Policeman' like no one else. Allie had a big old high pram that they would tie onto the back of the wagon when they shifted and travelled – it was really for taking out with them when they went calling, but when they travelled Cathy would climb into the pram and sing 'The Laughing Policeman' at the top of her voice.

There was no doing any good with Cathy. As we passed through towns and villages – where all Traveller children knew to behave and keep quiet – we would have to walk at the side of the pram with her, trying to keep her hushed. She was a big old gal, for she could do little work and would sit about for most of the day, but Allie and Joe spoilt her to bits.

After breakfast we all went out into the copses picking. Besides from the few scraps between me and our Alfie, we picked really well. We felt safe with Joe alongside us – we knew there were a lot of men living rough in the woods and copses, and we were always wary of them, for we never knew what frame of mind they might be in if we met them in the middle of the woods. People called them tramps, but me dad had talked to a few of them and was told sad stories about returning from the war to find that all they had owned was gone – including their wives and families – so they'd had no choice but to take to the roads.

It's always a cold time when we pick the flowers in early spring, and February can be a cruel month. It was having a good time with us on that morning, for we shivered as we bent down in the brambles to reach and pick the shy little flowers there. Each year we went through the same routine, for not only did it bring in a few shillings, but brightened up the lives of the house-dwellers that bought them.

"I hope my Lenard catches me a couple of shushies by the time we gets back," I heard me mam say to Allie, "make me a warm broth!"

"And I hope he thinks of me and Joe while he's at it," smiled Allie.

"He will, my Allie! He'll ketch enough to feed the village, if I know him."

She was right. Me dad and our two Jack Russells – Bizzie and Spider – often caught more than we needed just for ourselves. He'd have the butcher's shop in mind while he was out hunting, for the butcher, coalman and baker mush were often willing to buy the wild shushies that he caught. Sometimes they would follow our wagon as we travelled through a village, waiting for us to pull in to give the men orders for rabbits and other game they might catch, and our men were only too happy to oblige – so long as they could take the skins back after they had been prepared. There was money to be made in the skins as well as the meat, and so our men always took the opportunity to sell them twice.

We must have been in the copse a good couple of hours when we were called to stop. By then, we'd picked enough for the day to get out of the cold. Me poor little skinny legs felt like lumps of wood as I picked me way between the blackberry brambles to get out of the copse. I was stiff with cold, and our fire was a welcome sight – Jim had the kettle on the old kettle iron, already boiling, so tea was not long in coming.

We children bunched up together by the fire as our mams were busy getting the black pots ready for making broth. Jim said he would ride his horse back to the village and fetch new bread for the women.

"Well, you take this clean sack-bag to carry it all in," ordered me mam. "Otherwise the bread will end up all over the road – I know how you rides, Jim!"

"Yeah, better drunk than sober," Jim laughed before he rode off to the village. His horse was so well broke in that he rode it bareback, using just a halter, and we did the same with our own. None of us owned any fancy riding gear like saddles or bridles.

Me dad came back with his shushies and called to Alfie to tie up the dogs before they ran off on their own. Bizzie and Spider liked to play with the badgers, not realising that they weren't big enough to play or fight with them. We knew that badgers would fight to the death to protect their young, or if the dogs got into their sett.

Living our kind of life, we were always close to wild animals and grew to know the habits of them. You could say we lived with them, stopping as we did in the countryside, and many times me dad took us across a field or down a lane to watch the badger young at play, or a family of fox-cubs.

"You must creep quiet as mice, or they'll hear you and hide away," he would tell us. All young Traveller children got taught about nature, not just my family. We all knew how to look for and find hedgehogs, wild ducks, pheasants and partridges. We knew how to pick out the clean johnsnails[11] and work out if they were fit to eat. We knew that animals expecting young were not fit to eat, such as rabbits when in milk. By our customs, they are considered dirty, and so we knew which animals were fit for the pot depending on the time of year.

The smell of the shushi stew was grand as we children carried on bunching the snowdrops. An old fellow soon came past on a pushbike, stopping to tell us that he could smell the cooking way on up the road.

"Made me feel hungry," he said.

"You'd be welcome to a bit," me dad offered.

"Thank you all the same," he replied, "but my wife will have my dinner on the kitchen table, I hope!"

We smiled as he cycled on. Some people did stop to have a word with us, and we enjoyed it when they took the time to speak. Others would pass us by, keeping their eyes on the road or in the hedge, not even glancing at the side of the road where we were stopped. Me dad always said that it took all sorts to make the world. It wouldn't do for us all to be the same, would it?

As we ate out broth, it was decided that we could pick a few more

---

11. Romani name for snails found on walls.

snowdrops for Allie, to even up the bunches we would share, and then pull out come the morning. Joe raised his head.

"Did you just say we'll pull out in the morrow, Lenard?"

"I did, Joe," he replied, "is you hard of hearing?"

"No I ain't – but I bet you a shilling that we pulls out today!"

"Why's that then?" asked Allie.

Joe nodded to something in the distance. "Well, just look who's coming up the road." We looked to see a policeman approaching us on his pushbike.

"I was thinking to myself it was too good to be true," said Jim. "Nobody had been near us. It's your fault, May – that policeman's been and tracked the smell of your stew!"

"It's nothing to laugh at!" Joe scolded him. "I was enjoying the rest and the fire."

We waited until the policeman came to us, getting off his pushbike. "It's time you lot moved on," he said.

"We only just got here!" said Joe.

"Don't you tell me lies! You've been here two days now. It's time you were gone."

"We's gonna shift come morning, governor," me dad told him.

"You are all to be gone in an hour," the policeman ordered.

"Look," said Jim. "We come a long ways yesterday, and our horses needs the rest. We'll be gone a daylight tomorrow morning."

"Right then," the policeman said. "I'll be back at nine o'clock and if you're not gone I'll summon you to court. It's up to you."

We swore we'd be gone before then, and the policeman left feeling happy with himself for getting rid of the Gypsies.

The next morning we began to prepare for pulling back onto the road. We had to put out the fire and cover it with grass and pick up any rubbish to drop off on the next tip. We would head towards Gillingham, to Stourhead

Dilion, Amey and Betsy out calling with hawking baskets of wax roses.

Wood where we would pick the little wild daffies, but we knew they were a while away from being fit to pick. A couple of weeks would do the trick, and meanwhile we could take our time selling our snowdrop bunches.

When we reached the next village, Lilea and I went out with our mams and Aunt May to call on the doors. It was the first time that year we had gone calling, and so me dad pulled me aside to give me a strict warning.

"Maggie, my gal, when you go out today you will see money on the doorsteps. That money is not yours, Maggie. It belongs to the baker or the milkman or butcher, but not you. Now have you got that?"

"Yes, dad, I knows it," I replied.

"Well remember it, or you will get locked up!"

It was a familiar warning; he always gave us the same talk whenever we had to knock on doors, fearing that we would get ourselves into bother. We knew better than to pick anything up, but would accept a penny or two if some kind lady offered it. There were also the ladies who would set their dogs on you, or throw water at you just for opening the gate. You would meet all kinds while out calling, I can tell you; the good, the bad and the indifferent.

We were dressed up warm for the long walk ahead of us, me mam carrying the hawking basket full of flowers, and Lilea and I with our handfuls to sell. We worked well like this and I knew how to talk to the housewives at the doors.

"Can I sell you a bunch of lovely fresh flowers, mam?"

We would repeat it again and again through the day, and though so many people refused us, the snowdrops would sell. Snowdrops were such a popular wildflower, and though it took time to walk around the villages we were the first Travellers to have done so, as me dad had surmised. Pick first, sell first – that was his motto.

During the day Lilea and I had been given a few sweets and biscuits, but it didn't help the cold. We were dreading the long walk back to the wagons until May called out that she had sold her last bunch.

"Well, let's head back now so I can cook for my lot," said me mam. "I could eat me a grunt[12], I'm that hungry!" We all agreed and happily began to make tracks back along the road.

But all was not well when we arrived where we had stopped. Instead of seeing the welcome site of a roaring fire and our own wagons there was an empty space where they should have been! The police had been and moved them on, and all we found were lumps of grass left for us to follow, breadcrumbs to show us the roads our family had took.

We walked on till we reached a crossroads, counting the lumps of grass to choose the right road. Eventually we heard a horse coming towards us, and to our relief it was our own Patchie, being ridden hard by me dad. He put both me and Lilea up on the horse's warm back while he walked with our mams, explaining how they came to shift.

"He was a bloody swine, that policeman," we heard me dad say. "We

---

12. pig

told him that we was waiting for you, but he wouldn't listen – just made us go. Our Joe was going to knock him down."

"That would have helped matters with you three put inside for the next six months!" cried me mam. "Ain't you got no sense?"

"My Vie, I never said one word to that policeman," he soothed.

"Oh, I believes you, my Len. You probably said about a hundred words instead."

"She knows you, my Len!" laughed Allie, and me dad quickly changed the subject.

"Still," he said, "we got a good fire on for you, and the pots are simmering..."

"That's right, just think on your belly," said May. "All you brothers is the same! Your bellies comes first – don't worry about we three and the little 'uns walking the last ten miles!"

We must have walked a fair ways at that, I thought bitterly. We must have walked hundreds of miles a year – but it was a happy sight to see the wagons ahead of us, the smoke from the fire going straight up in the air.

As we waited for tea, me mam asked if anyone had thought where we were headed in the morrow, for we had enough flowers for another day's calling.

"Tell you what," said Jim, "you take it easy tonight. We'll shift in the morning and drop you off in the first big village we comes to."

All agreed that this was the thing to do, and me and Lilea shared the sweets we had gathered during the day amongst we children, keeping us all mates for the night.

We pulled out early and we five got dropped off for another day's work in a village near Shaftesbury. The wagons continued on, aiming for an out-of-the-way spot outside the village.

"Don't you go too far afield today, my Len," warned me mam as they left us to it.

We had a really good time calling, and one lady asked me mam to call back round on her way out of the village, promising that she had a few bits to give her for us children. When we returned to her, the woman gave her a lovely pram full of clean clothes and shoes for us, and treated us to cooked pigs' trotters. May and Allie had done well too, for they had munged[13] clothes for their lot and their basket was full of good togs and shoes for us.

When we got back to the stopping place, our boys' eyes lit up at the sight of the trotters.

In a way, I was a bit sad to see the last of that year's snowdrops, as I was so fond of those little flowers. We looked forward instead to picking the wild daffies.

---

13. begged

Chapter Five

Wild Daffodils

WE WANDERED UNTIL IT WAS MARCH. At least I guess we did, but times and dates meant very little to us. We didn't even have clocks, although everyone knew when it was time to fix up the wireless and listen to *The Archers* of an evening. We lived by the seasons and according to the state of the weather. It was the length of winter that set our time, as a hard, cold winter could put the first wild flowers back a few weeks.

At last we pulled up onto a narrow lane at Stourhead, near one of the biggest woods we went to in the course of the year. In the woods there was a huge house, which we had to give a wide berth to, but that never bothered me. I was more fascinated by the funny-looking house hidden away in the woods, known as 'the Convent'. It was made of stones put upon stones, and reminded me of when me dad would build his little rock walls on the Mendips.

We had to be careful of the gamekeeper, of course. He could hear a wagon and horse from a mile away, and knew that we Travellers would be after the flowers. We knew that he would come upon us soon enough, and so tied up all the dogs as we settled to wait for him. Soon, he came out of the woods and up to the fire, nodding as me dad called out to him.

"How are you, sir?" Me dad called everyone 'sir'.

"Fine, Len," he answered. He had his gun under his arm and his dog at his heel. "Is it that time of year already?"

"'Fraid so, sir. Can we pick a few daffies this year?"

"As long as you stick to my rules you can. I won't have my game disturbed, but you already know that."

"They won't get disturbed by my lot," me dad assured him. We were lucky that he knew the gamekeeper, as we were left to carry on picking as we liked as long as we didn't upset his pheasants, partridges or other game birds. Still, we took no chances to upset him, leaving the dogs tied up securely outside the woods and using pillowslips to hold the little daffies instead of our usual hawking baskets. We feared that he would stamp on them if we managed to upset him and we mightn't be able to replace them.

"Right, let's get on with it," said me mam once the gamekeeper had disappeared back into the wood. She turned to Alfie, Robert and myself. "If you three makes one squeak in them woods you won't be sitting down for a month. You do anything to upset that mush and you'll pay heavy!"

I looked to where Jimmy and Lilea were also being promised a slow death should they cause any trouble, and we children bit our lips as we were handed a pillowslip each and sent off deep into the wood, to where the pale yellow daffies spread out far and wide. Once we came to the daffodil beds, Ally turned to us with a scowl. "Now, don't you cough or break wind!"

I ask you, how could you not want to laugh at a warning like that? We understood we had to be careful though, and so was whispering to each other to mind the brambles and tread carefully. Those little thorns always managed to rip my legs, and so I was grateful for the quiet chatter. Me mam soon parted me from our Alfie, which was just as well, for there was no doubt that we would have got at it.

"Pick 'em as long in the stem as you can," she told us, sending Alfie one way and me another. "Now, get to it!"

These dense woods smelled so different to those copses where we had picked the snowdrops. In the dark copses there had been a damp, woody smell, but here there was a sweet aroma of herbs every time you trod upon the ground. You could smell the pine in the huge fir trees and notice the big sticky buds on the conker trees. "Not long afore spring comes," I thought to myself. How I loved the spring, when all the birds would be building their nests, and we would cover the ground looking for the first celandines – the little yellow flowers that greeted the new season. The primroses would be thinking of coming out and flowering from the mossy banks and hedgerows, keeping the sweet-smelling violets company. Yes, we had something grand to look forward to, just around the corner.

We picked until we'd had our fill and then quietly made our way out of the woods and back to the fire. Me mam reported our good behaviour to me dad before pulling out the tin baths to keep the daffies fresh.

It was a close-knit group of Travellers that sat round the fire that evening, making up bunches of daffies, backed by the evergreen box privet. Even the men joined in our task, for we had picked a lot of flowers. The wild daffodil is nothing like the garden sort, and they were delicate and pale in colour. We knew for sure these bunches would sell like lightning – just wait till the housewives saw the hawking baskets full of bright bunches and smelled the box privet.

We were full of good spirit, laughing round the campfire together. Joe turned to me dad with a smile. "We've been lucky again, Lenard. We must be the first ones hereabouts."

"If things goes on like this it could just be our lucky year," agreed me dad before turning to us all. "I've got to give it to you – you lot picked well today. Another day like this and we should have enough to last three or four days, or more!"

We went out again the next morning, and this time Joe came along with Ally. "Right you lot," he whispered, "heads down and arse up!"

We picked till our pillowslips were full and began to head back out of the woods. We heard strange noises, hollering and shouting, and thought at first someone was fighting – and getting closer! "Quick," one of our lot hissed, "let's make a run for it!"

As we ran we realised that it wasn't a fight, but a family unknown to us who were dashing and hollering. We never spoke, but kept going until we came out onto the lane. We came to a quick stop, for in front of us were our men, rounding on a group of strange Travellers.

"Put the daffies on the tail rack and start packing up," ordered me mam, and we hurried to obey her before a fight broke out.

Me dad was squaring up to a Traveller man we had not met before, whose family stood behind him shouting and bawling.

"You should have stopped and talked before you let your fools run wild in the wood," me dad was saying. He looked furious. "The gamekeeper's like to shoot your dogs and your children, you bloody good-for-nothing panch-mouth[14]!"

The other man bristled. "I'll teach you lot right from wrong. Put your dukes up!"

"You've ruined it for everybody now," Joe started, drawing himself up beside me dad. "Now none of the Travellers coming up behind us will be able to pick any flowers!"

We finished loading the wagons and me mam marched over to the group of men, telling me dad we had to shift before the policeman

14. An insult that makes reference to the panch or paunch of a sheep, the part of a sheep's stomach where it stores grass to be chewed later and which is considered dirty and needing much scrubbing before it can be cooked.

came. "And come he will, my Len!"

He seemed to calm down a bit at that and gestured for everyone to get a move on before leaning in to the stranger. "We'll meet again, mister, you and me."

Jim admitted that he too was worried about the gavvers[15] coming, and me dad turned back towards us. "Alright, let's fetch the horses and get going."

Even as he said it we heard a gun go off, and we rushed to get the wagons ready to leave. In no time the gang that had gone into the wood come running out like the devil himself was after them, and hard on their heels come the gamekeeper – and he was angry, alright.

"You've ruined months of my hard work," he hollered at me dad. "There's game scattered all over the woods, and those bloody dogs have killed my young pheasants!"

Me dad stepped forward at that. "Hang on a minute, sir, it had nothing to do with my lot. You knows my word is me bond – them's the people you want!"

The gamekeeper quickly turned on the other family, but me dad stayed by us while Jim and Joe fetched the horses. We were still harnessing up when two police officers arrived in a car, and suddenly there was bedlam! The unknown Travellers were screaming that the gamekeeper had tried to shoot their children and had shot the dogs.

We kept quiet, not saying a word while the gamekeeper explained to the police that he had let our family – who were known to him – into the woods to pick some flowers. We had behaved, he'd said. We'd done no harm. "Then this lot of hooligans rampaged through my woods and set their dogs loose on my game birds! I shot the dogs – as is my right!"

"Do you wish to press charges?" asked one of the policeman.

"Yes he do," answered me dad, still smarting from the broken-up fight. "Lock the lot of 'em up, the no-good bastards!"

---

15. police officers

"If I were you I'd go now while the going's good," warned the policeman, "or you could find yourself locked up an' all!"

"I ain't done nothing!" cried me dad.

"Lenard!" me mam shouted, and we all jumped. "Come on now, we's all a-ready."

But me dad had to have the last word, and looked at the Traveller man he'd been arguing with before. "I hope they locks you lot up and throws away the key. I'll be looking out for you, mister, you've spoilt it for everybody, you have."

"Not for you," the stranger said, "Not by the looks of all them daffies you got!"

"And you ain't got none, bloater-mouth!" laughed Joe as we set off, getting away from all the trouble as fast as we could.

Chapter Six

The Old Granny

WE LEFT ALL THE TROUBLE behind us, quick as we could, and travelled on to Shaftesbury Common, North Dorset. I always enjoyed stopping at that bit of common land, it was a good stopping place where we could be sure of meeting some nice, old-fashioned Travellers who came and went on the Common all year round.

As we pulled up in a lane for the night, Joe and Allie told us they planned to make their way onto Prince Lane come the morning. "I'll make me way back to visit the old couple," Joe said, and me dad nodded his understanding. The Prince Lane was owned by my granddad and Johnny Ayres, and was part of the old Roman Road between Dunkerton and Peasedown St John, on the outskirts of Bath. They had owned it for many years, and me granddad and the old Granny spent most of their time there as the poor old man suffered from the gout. The old Granny was still like a spring chicken and could out-walk most of her daughters-in-law when out calling.

Me and our Alfie could never stick the old woman. She never took to me mam or we children. She called me mam a gorgie because she was

Emmy with the old granny, cooking shussie stew on the Prince Lane.

from Devonshire and brought her own ways with her. She was always very different from me dad's lot. Me mam never wore the black pinnies like they would, never minded showing her ankles and would often carry her hawking basket by the side, instead of tucked into the crook of her arm.

She didn't look traditional the way me dad's side did either. It upset some of them that she would wear lipstick and powder and cut her lovely dark hair into a bob instead of wearing it in a long, thick plait as they did. Many of the others covered their heads with black scarves or hats, but not so me mam. I remember her letting her hair blow in the wind as she walked.

I don't remember her ever getting upset about what they all thought. She was her own person and refused to change just because they didn't like her ways, but what really upset her was the way the old woman would treat me and our Alfie.

The old Granny was a well-built woman, always dressed in deep black from head to toe, with a man's old trilby hat to top it all off. I try now to think of something nice to say about her, but she had the morals of a crab-apple tree, and was just as sour. She smoked a little clay pipe, drank like a fish and swore like a trooper. Oh, she was as mean as they come and had it in for me and our Alfie.

We hated it when we heard we had to stop with her. Me mam and dad, they warned us not to cheek her or answer her back, no matter what she told us two to do for her. We would fetch her wood and water – not just once or twice, but all day long, till we were ready to drop. She only treated me and Alfie like it – the other grandchildren got off easy!

Even when we were young, me granddad and Granny lived just the two of them, and so they couldn't get much with their ration books. Me mam gave them one of ours, to make things a little easier, and it just so happened to be mine. Many, many times, the old Granny would use the sweet coupons and eat every single one of them in front of me and Alfie. She would unwrap those boiled sweets while they were still in her pinnie pockets – we would hear the wrapper coming loose before she put them in her mouth.

Me mam, on the other hand, would never waste her sweet coupons, and would swap them instead for tea, cheese or mixed dried fruit to make spotty dicks. She would even use Parazone to bleach out the blue stamps that the shopkeepers marked the used coupons with so that they could be reused. That's how hard things were back then; no sweets for us.

We lot would cry for a sweet each as the old woman sucked away on them, only to get a clip round the ear for causing trouble!

Over the many visits we made to the old Granny, we two used to pray that her pipe would flare up. "Please Gawd, let that pipe burn me Granny's nose!" When she was on her deathbed, many years later, she asked for a last drag on her pipe. As one or t'other lit it, the clay pipe flared right up and burnt the hairs right out of her nostrils! Later, when he got back, me dad told me and Alfie that he had heard us whispering it over the years and now we had finally got our wish.

No, I never liked me Granny much at all. Now, the old granddad was a different kettle of fish. He was a lovely old man, a dear old boy who truly loved us all, whereas his wife was spiteful. I can still see her in me mind's eye, coming back down the Prince Lane as drunk as a hand-cart. She had gone out calling and stopped off at the Prince of Wales pub on her way home. At last she would appear, singing at the top of her voice, skirts flying and her old hat all shapes. If there was no one stopping with the two of them who could cook granddad a meal, he would get none at all when she was like this. She was very partial to a jug or two of brown ale and made sure she got it, never mind the poor old boy – he could do without!

Oh she was a mean old cow. Her favourite words were, "Fetch me this, fetch me that!" I can honestly say I never missed her when she went – and nor did many others!

On this occasion me dad decided we would not be turning back, but would instead work our way slowly to Bridgwater to wait for the peas and broad beans. Me and Alfie were more than relieved to hear him say it, though we would miss the company when we parted ways the next morning.

Me mam with baby Emily, taken in the Fifties in Trowbridge, Wiltshire.

So Joe and Allie went back and we finally arrived at Shaftesbury Common. We spotted a fair few wagons and tents, some belonging to the Maidments, Coopers and Hughes – all lovely old families who we knew well and who came to greet us as we arrived, giving advice about the best place to pull our wagons and where the horses could graze.

Once we were settled, me dad soon took our Ticker off with him, disappearing for days on end. Me dad and his horses had a secret life of their own and some things we were not allowed to know nothing about, but a few months after he had taken Ticker away we found out she was to have a foal – and that's all we knew about it. These parts of life were never spoken of in front of women and children.

While we waited for me dad to return, the men busied themselves making pegs and the women went out calling to sell them. Some of the families had traps and trolleys the women could use to go out in. We had sold our wild daffies, so mam took May out with them, but I was left to look after our little Emily – keeping her warm and fed up in the wagons and boiling up her towelling nappies in a bucket on the tire, ready for me mam to wash and hang on the bushes to dry.

Me Dad's brother Jessie with wife Louis, 1956.

Life went on this way until the end of March, when we set off for Shepton Mallet before moving on to Emborough Pond Lanes. Emborough Pond was a favourite stopping place of ours. Already some of the Ayres, Bowers and Smiths folk were gathered there, with some of me dad's lot – Jessie and Louie and their children – whiling away the time till the pea-picking could begin in May.

In the lanes there were wagons of all shapes and sizes: barrow tops, square bows, readings, all painted in nice bright colours, with a few traps and trolleys to share between the families for calling or trips to the pub at night. It made for a grand site.

We children could run and play, and although we were told not to go near the big pond they were the very first place we ran to. It was a great place to play, for around the pond were enormous trees and bushes to muck around in until we were missed, and me dad would come riding up on one of the horses, hollering at us to get back to the wagons. Come the end of summer, when we would set out again, the men would often swim in the ponds – but we were never allowed for fear we would drown.

It was funny, for though we could never see any danger, the grown-ups were always on at us. The things they would come out with!

"If you goes and kills yourself," they would tell us, "don't you come running back to me!"

Chapter Seven

The Swine's Jump Road

IN THE COMPANY OF HIS OLD FRIENDS and family, me dad went out drinking most nights. Me mam, to get him away from the other men, talked him into shifting down to Glastonbury for a while, and his brother Jessie and his lot came along too.

I remember how much we enjoyed going through Wells. We pulled up in the town itself, right in front of the shops, all bright and handsome. It was so busy and full of life, and on each side of the street a little stream of water flowed down the road. People stopped and stared at us but no matter. We were used to it.

One man shouted out, "Hey-up, the Gypos are in town!"

"What's it to you?" Me dad matched his volume.

"Leave the man be," chided Jessie, just as loud. "He ain't right in the head."

The man, knowing he had bitten off more than he could chew, strode off down the street – looking back over his shoulder to make sure "they Gypos" never followed him (me dad probably would have an' all, given half a chance).

We travelled on to a well-known stopping place we called Dicky's

Copse. It was on the edge of the moor just outside the little village of Street. There was a fresh-water stream on the lane itself, so we didn't have to beg for water. For this reason, most of our stopping places had streams nearby. They were found many generations ago, and we rely on them wherever we travel.

Not long after we had pulled in, the police came out from Glastonbury.

"How long do you intend to stay here, then?" they asked.

"A couple of weeks," Jessie answered. "We's just waiting to pull onto the pea fields."

The policemen knew only too well why we were there, and we knew they would let us be for now. "Just make sure you leave no rubbish behind."

We agreed gladly, happy not to have been moved on. From there, we could easily walk to the outlying villages to sell pegs and go calling. Ashcott, Glastonbury, Meare and many others were all a comfortable distance away. We children also knew that we were near the Swine's Jump, and couldn't wait to be told the old tale as we travelled through it in a few weeks' time, shivering and shaking with fright and excitement.

There were now three of our wagons travelling together to the pea-fields at North Petherton and so we knew we had to get there early in order to book in. We were hoping to work for Mr Williams, but each year there were more and more Travellers looking to pick the beans and peas in Somerset. Me mam hoped he might let us in the paddock so we could get off the road, for we had a lot of children to keep fed and warm between our three families.

Of course, as soon as we heard this we children began to make plans of our own, for we knew which orchard got the Morgan sweet apple trees in it, and though they would still be in blossom we would mark them out as ours and pick to our hearts' content come August, when they were full and ripe. The Morgans were so sweet that it was better than a bag of sherbet, so we would keep an eye on they trees!

Soon enough, we set off to North Petherton and approached the very road we children had been waiting for as soon as we had found out our destination. The village of Ashcott is on the main road to Bridgwater and not far outside the village is a dark wood – a thick, dense, damp area where very few flowers could grow – known as Loxley Wood to the locals. We knew it as the Swine's Jump Road.

"Oh dad, tell us about the Swine's Jump," we would whine, almost as soon as we were past the village. We knew the children in the other wagons were asking the exact same thing. "Go on, dad, tell us!"

"Alright," he would laugh, preparing the story. "Set yourselves down and be quiet!"

This is the old tale that has been handed down through my people for many years:

Years ago, there was a bad murder committed around the Glastonbury area, and the man who killed the other was fierce and cruel. He was to be tried at the assizes in Bridgwater and so the police were forced to travel with him from the lock-up in Glastonbury to Bridgwater.

Fearing the man's cruelty, they bound his hands and his feet and placed him in a horse and cart to make the long way to his trial. It would be a weary journey at the horse's slow pace.

At a certain point, the police stopped the cart on a narrow road in the middle of a dark, barren wood to give the horse a rest. While they sat chatting, the murderer, still bound hand and foot, leapt from the back of the cart, took three long jumps towards the trees and disappeared into the dense, dark woods.

The policemen searched through the night and the morning, inside the woods and out, but although they looked hard the man was never seen again. He became known as the 'Swine', and the Travellers of the day christened the wood 'the Swine's Jump Road'.

This was a tale that always gave us shivers as we travelled through those dense woods, looking out for the Swine still haunting his escape. We would ask me dad to keep repeating it to us, over and over again, until long after we'd passed through those creepy woods.

The trees around us were old and bowed, meeting over the road so that it seemed we were moving through a dark tunnel. We knew, though, that we were safe with all the family around us. It was nice to feel safe and secure, to be loved like the children we were, but we hungered for the thrill of the old ghost tales that the generations handed down.

I have always felt that we Romanies are a mystic race; we seem to know nature and feel things like no one else. Our Alfie was very deep-minded and was able to see or feel things that had happened in the past and present. Once in a while he would prove his mystic mind, such as when we were travelling down roads we'd never travelled before and he would tell me dad what was round the next bend in the road, though we never truly realised it until he was about eleven years old. There were some old stopping places that we gave a wide berth to, where misdeeds and murders had been done. Although the details of what might have happened on certain roads had been lost, the old ones still knew about the bad places, where a soul or spirit was not at rest, and we would leave these places well alone.

Too soon we pulled up in the town of Bridgwater. We set down along the riverside just off the main street while the women all went off shopping.

"Don't forget to get me a bit of baccy, Vie," me dad called out.

"You haven't earned any yet," she called back, laughing as she went. We all knew she would get him some, if only to keep the peace.

All along the riverbank there were lovely shops lined up: bakers, butchers, clothes shops with pretty ribbons and hairslides. The smell of the hot bread and cooked pigs' trotters and tripe made us feel starving. The shops looked handsome. I turned to me dad.

"Can I go and look in the shop winders, dad?"

"Only as far as I can see you," he agreed. "In case we get moved on."

The people were used to seeing us Travellers come to town each year, so did not take much notice of us. That in itself was nice. In fact, some of the house-dwellers would be coming out on the fields to earn a few shillings themselves. By the look of them, some of them needed it. I saw one poor woman pushing a big old pram with at least three little ones stuffed in it, and others hung onto the pram or her skirts, looking like ragged robins. There are a lot worse off than we were.

Me dad noticed her too and turned to his brother Jessie. "I bet that one lost her man in the war. She looks as poor as a church mouse, and with that big family."

"Well, look again," said Jessie. "If she lost her man in the war, who gived her they little 'uns then?"

"Sure enough," sighed me dad. "She may have a man somewheres, but we should give her a shilling to buy they children some bread."

Jessie nodded and called out to the woman. "Missus! Hey, Missus! Here a minute."

"I can't buy any pegs," she replied.

"We don't want you to," said me dad. "Have you got bread money for they little 'uns?"

The poor, dear woman only looked at them, probably thinking they were about to rob her.

"Here, take this and feed your brood." Jessie took more coppers off me dad and handed her a fistful of change. She was overcome, thanking them over and over.

"It ain't all the world," laughed me dad, "but be sure to spend it on grub for they children, missus!"

Oh, if there is one thing we couldn't stand, it was to see hungry children. It just pulled at our heartstrings. They never said a word about giving the money to the woman, though our mams would never have minded – it was just how things were done.

Chapter Eight

Pea-Picking Time

IT FELT GOOD TO ARRIVE at North Petherton, for we knew we had weeks on end till the pea-picking would end and we knew we had a place to live and work for the whole time. The paddock we were stopping in had a tap for water, and there was a huge pile of wood in the farmyard for us to use.

There was also a sandy-bottomed stream nearby, that we children spent many a happy hour playing in. Me mam always warned us to be careful, hollering at us as we left, "If you gets yourselves drowned, don't come crying to me!" We had to laugh – and they wondered why we had no sense!

Mr Williams was as pleased to see us as we were to see him. He invited us to pull in and pick our spot, and our parents chose near the side of the little stream – better to keep their eyes on we lot! Oh we did love to splash and play in that clear water, and me mam would rinse her washing in it, and dip it out to wash our hair in. It felt cleaner than the tap water and fresher.

Over the next few days more and more wagons pulled in to Mr

Pea-picking towards the end of the War at Williams Farm, North Petherton,
Bridgwater: mam, me and Robert with some of the gorgie pea-pickers.

Williams' fields, letting the horses stretch their legs as they settled in. We
saw the Meadens, Ayres, Bowers, Penfolds and Broadways, and me
dad's lot came in twos and threes until we had all the pickers we would
need. Mr Williams wasn't the only pea-farmer in the area, of course,
and over the years we picked for all of them. Hundreds of wagons
travelled to this area at the end of May.

The big day finally came round, and the peas were declared fit to pick.
That Monday morning we were all lined up on the edge of the pea field
with a heap of nets to put our pickings in. Each family was given a
number of nets, all of which had to weigh twenty pounds, and these
were counted off each week for pay day. The farmer's boy would come
out on the field several times a day to weigh off the nets of peas and
take them back to the farmyard for packing.

As the Travellers in the line started to pick there was much leg-
pulling and joking over who would reach the far hedge first. Picking our

way across the field in straight lines was the easiest way to make sure we didn't miss any, for the peas were grown in rows. But woe betide anyone who snatched at the peas in someone else's row on the way across, and if you got ahead of the others you had to be sure to throw the leftover vine behind you and not on someone else's patch.

To pick peas, you must pull out the whole plant, pick off each of the little peas and then throw down the useless vine to be ploughed back into the ground at a later date. This helped to clear the ground as we went along and made sure we didn't miss anything. The grown-ups picked from the first peep of daylight, going back for breakfast at around six or seven, when we children would join them. It was great fun, that first day. Me and our Alfie had our own net each and would race against each other to see who could fill their bag first. There was a knack to it, and any peas over the twenty pounds per bag were given back to the picker, so we always tried to put a few extra handfuls into each.

I was happy out in the peas and would sometimes follow me mam and dad out on the peas at dawn while our Alfie was lighting the fire for breakfast. It was chilly early in the mornings, but nice to pick and listen to the birds singing away. We would have to watch out for the old rooks who liked the lush peas for breakfast, though the farmers had put up fierce looking morkins.[16]

Those morkins proved to have more than one use that year, mind. My Aunt May struggled to get up in the early morning. She liked to lay a-bed till eight or nine while the rest of the family were picking from four am. Jim had been trying for weeks to get her up with the rest of us and this one morning he'd had enough – so he stuffed dry pea-vine up the little Queenie stove chimney and lit the fire in their wagon. The smoke billowed out of their wagon and me Aunt May flew from the door, screaming fit to burst. When she found everyone standing about laughing, she and Jim got at it.

---

16. scarecrows

"Now you'll get out of bed in they mornings," he hollered at her.

"I shan't pick another pea this year!" swore May.

"You will!" Jim stalked out into the peas and picked up one of the morkins, beating her up and down the field with it! We were in an uproar till one or t'other put a stop to it. She was up bright and early the following morning and every morning after. We still talk of it to this day: the day Jim beat poor May with a morkin, its arms swinging every which way. I remember me dad turning to me mam with a cheeky laugh.

"Now then, Vie, you knows what's in store if you don't get up early enough."

"And I'll warn you, my Lenard, that if you thinks I'll take that lying down you're wrong. I'd make you swallow it!"

What stunned everyone was that it was so out of character for Jim to beat May. He was one of the placid brothers and avoided any kind of violence. I love me Uncle Jim dearly.

Saturday was 'play day' for the grown-ups. The families would all leave in their finery to meet up in Bridgwater to shop and drink, while we children minded the wagons and young 'uns. Picnics of food and treats were left out for us, providing we didn't touch or open the food hampers in the wagons. We had to keep a close eye on the hampers because some of the other Traveller children would raid some other family's food hamper if they thought they could get away with it. Our cousin Lilea was one of them! She had a very sweet tooth and would go after the tin of sweet milk in me mam's hamper, dipping her fingers into the tin and getting sticky milk over everything. She enjoyed the treat while I would get beat for letting her do it, so I made sure Lilea was always in me sights – and I knew just how slippery that one could be!

When our parents returned, many of the men would be hanging on the carts or trolleys for grim death, and a few of the women likewise, singing at the top of their voices:

If I had my way, dear
You would never grow old
And sunshine I'd bring every day.

You would reign all alone
Like a queen on a throne
If I had my way.

They would pull out the step-board for dancing and, taking turns, would sing and dance by the light of the fire for half the night. Even though we couldn't make out too much of what they were talking about, we found it all so enjoyable and entertaining. The only sting in the tail was that, most Sundays, peas had to be picked for the Monday markets, so they would get very little sleep before they had to be out, shivering in the early morning air and grumbling for all they were worth.

Me mam seemed to take joy in it. "That lush does you a lot of good, eh Lenard?" she would say as me dad stumbled out into the peas with a bundle of nets beneath his arm. "You'll never learn, will you?"

"Shut up, my Vie, I'm dying."

"Well, die picking peas!"

"You cannot love me, or you'd let me off today," he'd moan pitifully.

"Get yourself out there and love they peas," mam would laugh.

Saturday was also our treat day. Sometimes we would get a little bag of sprats to fry as we wanted, or a pig's trotter each, or a sticky lardy cake to share. This was our pay for pea-picking all week, and we looked forwards to these treats each Saturday as much as the grown-ups looked forward to theirs.

That year, the weather was definitely on our side – long, hot, sunny days. Some years we got mixed weather with lots of rain, and then it was hard work as the plough field turned to thick, heavy mud that stuck

Pea-picking time: five mothers, including me mam in the middle, with their little army of pickers. Little Jessie is looking back at mam. This is the only photo we have of him. He died less than a year later.

to our boots and weighed a ton. We would drag our feet along the rows and got wet through to our skins.

Me mam was glad that year to have the little pram she had munged from a house-dweller those months back, for it meant our little Emily could come out onto the fields with us. There were prams dotted all over the field, as many families had small children. It could be hard work, dragging those heavy prams over the pea vine, but it was better to us than leaving the little 'uns back with the wagons while we moved across the pea and bean fields.

Many of us were born out on the pea fields. I was born on the pea field at Thurloxton, just up the road towards Bridgwater, so I felt right at home in the peas. Me dad always said that the best pickers were born in the fields, but I knew that was a load of bull to get me to pick faster. He must have thought me daft.

The faster pickers soon got ahead of the line, nets starting to pile up behind them. No one would ever touch another family's nets. We respected each other's hard work, and thieving amongst ourselves was never tolerated. The punishment was in the ruined name and reputation, which effectively meant banishment as it would be the end of their pea-picking season anywhere. We have our own rules to deal with wrong-doers. Fights and feuds could last for many generations as nothing was ever forgotten or forgiven, but on the whole we are a peaceful lot.

Come dinner time, our Alfie was sent back to the hedge where we had left the hamper, pots and pans, to light the fire so that we could have a fry-up and a break. All the young boys had this task and never minded it, for it got them away from the peas for a time. When the kettle was on the fire he would call us back and we would be there just long enough to eat and rest before heading back to the nets.

The first week of this work would cause problems for some. The constant labour could cause swelling of the hands and arms – we knew it as 'pea gout'. It was very painful, and treated with tight bandages or strips of cloth wrapped around the hand and arms until it healed. Another problem was stiff muscles and bad backs from bending over for so long. Despite this, each day was a delight in some way or another.

Like the hop-picking, it was a time for old friends and family to catch up and young couples to meet up and start courting, and a few weddings were booked up too while so many of us were in the same place for weeks on end.

We were doing fine that year, making each day count before it slipped away to the next. I would hear me dad call to me hundreds of times each day, "Come along, Maggie, pick on," and when that didn't work, "Pick on, my Maggie, and I'll get you a treat come Saturday."

Of course, come Saturday he would be in the pub with the other men, and my treat would go down the pan along with some of our hard-earned money – but me mam would make sure most of it was tucked safely in her pocket.

So many of the women were the same, letting their men think they were the big 'I Am', and all the while saving a few pounds here and there. We heard it all round the fires when the men were out of earshot.

"My man ain't got the sense he was born with," one would say.

"His mum must've dropped him on his head when he was born," said another.

They could be so funny at times, even as they took themselves and life so seriously. It fell on both parents to provide for the family – working hard on the fields or craft-making and calling – but the men often seemed to think it was their right to rule, and the rows between couples could sometimes get bloody. The men could be heavy-handed and beat their wives. I made up me mind at a very early age that when I grew up I would not take me a Traveller man for a husband. They seemed far too controlling for my way of thinking; too quick with their fists, and me dad always said I had a mind of me own. The black eyes I saw on women around me, growing up, was more than enough to make my decision by.

When things ran smoothly, though, life was often fun. We would sing around the fires and lay out the step-boards to dance on. Singing is a natural part of our way of life, whether in the evening or on the pea fields. Someone would begin softly, barely realising their own song, and others would join in with the lovely chorus. Some would chat to each other like baby magpies, calling across the music to catch up on the latest news. How I loved to just pick and listen, feeling so secure with our big group together as one.

Late into the morning the farmer would bring the town and village pickers to the fields, dropping them off on the back of a lorry. Some of these people would keep to themselves, while those who had grown to know us over the years would have a bit of fun with us.

At the end of the day we would collect a few peas for our supper and head back towards the paddock to shell them, while me mam did the

Pea-picking time. Taken in June 1943 in Jim Cole's paddock, Bridgwater: me mam, me and our Alfie.

washing for the next day's clothes. It was my job to peel the tatters and onions for me mam to fry with the thick-bellied pork.

How I hated they onions. We ate them with nearly every meal to keep illness away. There must be something in the old belief, for we Travellers never seemed to get bad or ill. I would eat raw onion with bread and cheese, but couldn't stand it cooked or fried and would spend most of me meals picking it out, cussing like a drayman.

When the day's work was done, the men would sit in a big group chatting and playing cards while the women – and me mam was the worst – washed their children's hands and faces in a tub by the fire. We would all cry as the carbolic soap got in our eyes and up our noses, stinging for a long time after, but if she'd had her way me mam would've washed us to death. Every chance she got we were put in that tub.

Once we had cleared the first pea field it was the turn of the broad beans. We had three big fields of them to pick before we could get back onto the peas, and I found them much harder even though the nets filled quicker. The bean fields had a different smell to the peas, for the late blossom was sweeter.

We moved off the paddock to be closer to the bean fields, and all me dad's family came with us the evening before we were to start on the new field. We children were back to fetching wood and water each night for the next day as we were no longer near that pretty little stream. We did have permission to take beans for ourselves to eat though, and this was a real treat for I would eat them cold and hot. We would eat the broad bean for a fortnight or so, and once they were gone I would be longing for them for another year. We Travellers lived well compared to most house-dwellers, for we had more chance at all the vegetables and fruit that we picked or cut despite the back-breaking hours we had to work to get them. Then we had all the wild rabbits, ducks and pheasants to catch for our meat.

Another drawback to working this time of year was that, no matter how hard we tried to avoid them, the wild poppies grew in abundance among the beans and peas and gave everyone a headache. They were a grand sight, though, bright red heads dancing in the breeze. If only they were kinder to us! Many of these fields were also used for the tatter crops and so we would sometimes find the odd young tatter that we could take back for our tea.

But all good things must come to an end and we had completed a good working season. We had planned to stay round Bridgwater for the fair and then head back up-country for the hops, but me mam had a change of heart, suspecting that me dad would get through most of our hard-earned money if he was given the chance at the horse fair. Instead, we were going straight on to Ledbury.

It was a shame for we loved the fair nearly as much as me dad did, but for once he gave in to Little Fiance's wishes and we headed towards Radstock where we would call in to see the old granny and granddad.

Chapter Nine

The Prince Lane

WHEN WE HEARD WE WERE OFF to visit the old granny, Alfie and I couldn't help but look at each other. Here we go again, we both thought, not looking forward to this visit one little bit.

"Do we have to?" asked me mam.

"I ain't set eyes on them for months," answered me dad, though even he seemed reluctant. "I must, my Vie."

"Well I hope she leaves me children alone, or this time I'm bound to tell her!"

"One night, that's all. Just one night and then we'll shift on."

"Make sure we do," me mam told him. "I knows your old mother."

They went back and forth between them for a while.

"What can I do?" asked me dad. "If I rows with her it'll upset the rest of my lot and then there'll be rows all round."

"I know, my Len," me mam said softly, "but it's hard for me to watch my children being put on all the time. Our Maggie and Alfie have got to hate that old woman, and it ain't right, when we've done our best to give 'em manners..."

"Give over now, my Vie," begged me dad. "Sing us a song."

At least we two knew then that our mam would stick up for us against the old granny – and me dad would as well, if pushed. Me mam started to sing, and we settled down to travel along the well-known roads as we liked best.

Cold blows the blossom, down falls the snow
Left in the wide world was poor little Joe,
No mother to guide him, for in the grave she lay low.
Left to wander was poor little Joe.

A carriage came by, with a lady inside,
Look at poor Joey a-running behind.
She threw him a penny to buy him some bread,
And as he was running, he wished himself dead.

Cold blows the blossom, down falls the snow
Left in the wide world was poor little Joe
No mother to guide him, for in the grave she lay low
There's no one to care for poor little Joe.

We could hear Jim and May aside us, picking up the tune and singing along to the sound of the horses' feet and the wagons' wheels on the hard mud beneath us. Everyone was happy as we travelled through Westonzoyland, where there was a bit of common land left over from the army during the war. It had cement roads and a few huts still intact and made for a good stopping place for a few days.

From there, we went on to the little lane under the Glastonbury Tor. It had lots of fresh springs of clean water and the old hedges were full of dry wood for the fires. This was such a favourite stopping place for Travellers that years later it was named 'Gypsy Lane'. It was well used because the police didn't seem bothered that we would stop there, and we could easily walk to Glastonbury for the shops. There was the added treat that we children could run up the steep fields of the tor and roll all the way back down!

From there we went up through Shepton Mallet and down to Binegar Bottom – which we always called Vinegar Bottom. The next day saw us reach Peasedown St John, where we stopped in the village to pick up a few things before heading down the lane that would take us past the Prince of Wales pub and towards the Prince Lane – and sure enough, there in the lane stood the old granny, poking her skimmer in the cooking pot.

By the smell of it, she had herself a rabbit broth on the go, and it did smell kushtie.

"You lot stick close to the wagon," we were told, "and don't cause any trouble!"

The greetings began as they always did, with the granny asking me dad if he had got himself lost. "You ain't shown your face in months," she said. "We could all be dead and buried for all you lot cares."

"You got a gab on you, old woman. You ain't never satisfied." We could tell me dad was disappointed, but at least granddad was pleased to see us all.

"Have you done yourselves a good bit of pea-picking?" he asked us, meaning, of course, had we earned plenty of money?

"We never done too bad," smiled me dad.

"Did you bring us a meal of peas back?" snapped the old granny, at the same time hoping that we hadn't.

"Yes, of course." Me mam pointed towards our wagon. "They's on the tail rack."

"Now stop grumbling, woman," said granddad, as our granny inspected the bag of peas we had brought with us. "They thought of us, that's for sure."

"That makes a change, Dannal, for they to think on we lot, stuck here in the lane. If they worried about me and you then we'd see a lot more of 'em."

Finally granddad snapped at her. "Shut that gab of your'n, Emma, and let the man be!"

That quieted her for a while, but we knew she would probably put the blame on me mam for us not coming back sooner. It was easy to blame me mam, though never in front of her face.

Once we had said our greetings, we went to see who else was in the lane. My dad's eldest brother Tom and his wife Kizzie were both there and they were glad to see us. He was a very quiet man who loved to have a gang of children around him.

He was in the early stages of that dreaded disease tuberculosis, but that never stopped us from throwing our arms around his long legs in a warm hug.

Of course, our joy couldn't last, and it wasn't long before we heard the old granny calling out to us. "Lenard, get they young 'uns to fetch me some wood and a can of water."

"I'll fetch you some meself in a bit," he called back with a wink at us. "My lot have just walked up from Radstock. Wait till I see to me grys and then I'll fetch whatever you wants. Will that satisfy?"

How that old woman loved a good grumble. Nothing ever satisfied her. They all sat round the fire talking and catching up for half the night, for me mam said the old woman was up for a row and so we had better start on the long road to Ledbury come the morrow.

Me and our Alfie would have dearly loved to have taken granddad with us, but the old man's gout was on him again. Anyway, he would never leave his old Emma, however much we would have liked to take him along with us. Like me Uncle Tom, our granddad had plenty of time for us little 'uns. He was always showing us how to make things that would earn us a living when we were grown, and repeating the old fireside tales that we so loved to hear.

Looking back on this time of my life, I think this must have been our Romani way – the old ones teaching their skills to the young – for this way we never forgot. If I'd had a nice granny, maybe I would've learned her old skills in flower-making and cooking, but she was the kind you could never approach, and in fact we hid from her most of the time. All the same, it would have been nice as me mam's family and me dad's both lived a different lifestyle, and it would've been nice to have the best of both.

Chapter Ten

Dad's Magic Flowers

T HE NEXT MORNING WE SAID FAREWELL once again and pulled out of the Prince Lane towards Ledbury and the hop gardens, with Jim and May following on behind. We were heading towards Bristol so that we could follow the old Gloucester road to Ledbury. They were roads and lanes that our family knew well, having made this very same journey each year for generations. We knew each fast-running brook and farmer's trough where we could find safe, clean water – we had to know these things, for most folks in houses wouldn't let us mung any of their tap water. Looking back, it seems a sad life in which you couldn't beg a kettle of water, but that was the way of things then, I suppose.

It was the time of year when the family made and sold wooden flowers. Me dad used to make delicate chrysanthemums from elder bush – big, beautiful blooms that shone snow-white when they were first made. I used to think of them as me dad's magic flowers.

We were all involved in the making of them. We young ones would go out with dad and Jim into the woods to pick out the sticks of elder bush that would be used to make the flower heads. We had to make sure they were the same thickness so that the flowers were all the same size. They were more beautiful that way.

When we got back to the fire we helped to strip all the skin off the elder sticks, making sure not to let any of the wood get into the fire. There's an old Romani belief that burning elder wood or ivy would bring bad luck upon the family, and we considered it wicked to do so. Once the sticks were all stripped me dad began to shave them, shaping them into the petals, with an old, sharp peg knife[17] – and it was sharp! Like all the men, me dad kept a whetstone which he was forever using to sharpen that old knife.

Gripping the stick, he would start to shave the end into a narrow point, to better marry the flower head to the evergreen privet. Then he shaved slivers from the end of the stick, creating curly petals out of the wood. The dozens of flower heads piled up and we put them by the fire to dry and harden. The smell that came from them was grand!

When they were dry, the women would dye them using different colour crepe paper. We would use red, yellow, pink and leave some of the little heads white. We would soak the paper in a bowl or bucket of warm water, and then dip in the wooden flower heads and shake them before leaving them out to dry again. Finally, we would shove the ends of the privet up into the head to make the stems.

The large, brightly coloured heads showed up handsomely in the hawking baskets, and so they always sold well. They were a beautiful sight when married together and arranged in their little wooden bunches, and if their water was changed regularly the evergreen privet would take root in the water and stay fresh for months.

I enjoyed this time of year, for most days we stopped in a different field or lane, sometimes veering off to new villages where new sights could be seen. We were never allowed to wander far from our parents,

---

17. A small, wooden-handled knife used for shaping wood to make pegs, baskets, etc.

though, but always warned to stay where we could be seen and heard.

With our flowers made up, we went out calling every day. We were moved on a few times by the village policemen, but each day took us closer to the hop gardens and the weeks of peace we knew awaited us, where all the old family and friends would be together once more. I knew our Alfie would soon be bending me ear, telling me how to behave meself and to leave him be.

"I'm playing with the boys," he'd soon be saying, little mush thinking he was a man already, "so don't follow me, my Maggie!"

As if I would.

Apart from picking the hops, during the day we would have such fun, especially in the evenings when everyone would let themselves go, singing and dancing on the boards. So roll on the miles, we would say each day. Let's get to it!

I knew me dad and Jim could taste the brown ale and beer already, for each Saturday night – just as in the pea-picking season – they would be off up the pub with all those other men.

As we neared the fields, we children would sit by the fire at night and listen to the tales of hop-picking when our parents were young. Who ran away with whom; who had a good clean fist-fight; who bought the prettiest bit of ware. It seemed like nothing was forgotten.

Me dad and Jim had many stories of the boxing matches and fighting games that went on during the hop-picking seasons. Though a peaceful people for the most part, there were many Traveller men who would travel miles to watch a good fist-fight. Whoever could fight the longest and best and stay fair and inside the rules was considered the winner.

The men often witnessed these fights and told the story to the whole family later around the fire. Some fights lasted so long and been that bloody that they have gone down in our history. One such fight was between a young unknown named Freddie Mills, who was beaten by Young John Small at Tipton St John, near Exeter.

It was me mam that brought the tale up to the Travellers in Wiltshire, for Freddie Mills became the world light heavyweight boxing champion in 1948–50, and so for John Small – a close relative of me mam – to have beaten him so squarely was like having an important bit of history for ourselves.

Chapter Eleven

The Hop Gardens

AT LAST WE REACHED THE HOP GARDENS, looking for familiar faces, wagons and horses as we pulled through the gateway. We were never the first to arrive on this farm. Some families began their work months before we arrived, tying the hop vines to the thin poles that held them as they grew. Their season was a much longer one than ours.

Some of me dad's brothers were already settled in, with fires flaring up and black pots boiling. The smell of stew cooking away welcomed us from most parts of the big field. We was full of excitement as we took in what was to be our working and stopping place for the next five weeks: all these lovely families from all parts of the country, scattered over the field in tents of all shapes and wagons of all colours. Those without wagons had trolleys covered over with green canvas sheets, to make sleeping places for their children that were warm and dry. We were a mixed crew from all walks of life. We had our well-off Travellers alongside those not so well-off, and the poor Travellers who worked like dogs but never seemed to have anything to show for it. What we all shared was the family around us – each of our families was a tight unit, and no matter how little we had we worked hard to make our homes inviting for others.

We had no choice but to take our time unhitching the wagon – me dad was approached from all sides, shaking the hands of people he knew and people he didn't, and there was much laughing and joking as we settled in. We would have a few days yet afore we started to pick our first hops, time to find our old warm clothes – boots and wellies – for if it did happen to rain we would know it! We'd be in for a hard time with the mud clinging to us, as well we knew from past years, and so we piled up our warm clothes and boots just in case, with enough spare for those children that had none themselves, or very little. The farmer had put piles of wood out for our fires, and there was a tap for water which saved us a lot of time. We could get eggs, butter and milk from the farm, so all in all we were set. The hop farmers looked after their pickers as well as making money out of us, but it was work we needed badly.

Come Monday there would only be the very old and very young left on the field. The rest of us would be heading out to pick, packed with prams, food hampers, pots, kettles and a good old frying pan, ready to break ourselves into the work. We considered ourselves lucky compared to the house-dwellers who had come from the big towns to help pick. All they had to survive on was what they could carry on their buses or trains. They had very little compared to us, and had to live and sleep in barns or cowsheds, lucky if they had so much as a Primus stove to heat their food on.

We had our homes with us and, come Monday, the men of our group had a ritual to perform – for if there was one good deed they did each year, it was to see that every child on that field was fed and well, including those of the big town pickers.

Although the weather was dry, the October mornings left us shivering. We were woken early, before dawn, to get out of our warm beds and head to the cold, dark hop garden amid the grown-ups' cries of encouragement.

*Hop-picking at Ledbury: from left to right, Lilea, Sibby Ayres, Jimmy,
aunt May, uncle Jim and Checkers.*

"Come on, my babbies," called me mam. "It's time to put your shoulder to the wheel! There's no turning back – off to work we go!"

To say that all we children were sleepy and grumpy in the hop garden that first early morning was an understatement. Our parents took turns alternately begging, petting, praying and threatening us to pick the hops – and of course there were the usual cajoling promises of Saturday treats. If we'd been bought all the things promised to us we'd have needed a second wagon just to carry it all, but that was me dad all over.

The gardens were very dense for the hops grew up very high poles. We pickers spread up and down the rows of them. It was like working under a high hedge.

The hops were picked and placed in cribs made up of a wooden frame and sacking. They were weighed off by the bushel and the farmer would dip that old basket of his into the crib two or three time a day to weigh our work off against our daily target of bushels. He would tell us how we were doing, but it was never enough for me dad. It was a huge bonus for the family if the children picked their share of hops, speeding up the process and getting far more done, and so we all helped from an early age. Me dad would sit me down on the side of the crib and pull the vines down for me to pick bare. Our Alfie was finally tall enough to pull his own down.

The hops weren't nice to pick, for the vines had hundreds of prickly bits growing on them that ripped the skin from our faces and arms as we pulled them down from the poles. The vines left our hands with a green-yellow stain and smelled like no other plant, a very strong and bitter smell that got right into our skin. We stunk of them after a few days, but me mam insisted that it was a clean stink.

As the day warmed up a little the hop-dogs[18] began to come out on the move. Hop-dogs are the large, furry caterpillars that live on the hop leaves. The bright yellow and green caterpillars were much prized by we children – if we found one be sure that we hung onto it!

"Hop-dop! Hop-dog!" the shout came from one of the children, and me and our Alfie both stopped picking. "I got a hop-dog!"

We ran as fast as we could through the rows of hops to the crib where the caterpillar had been found, to find that many other children had done the same. Too many sticky little hands made a grab for it, and tears flowed from the child who had found it and made the mistake of shouting out, as the little hop-dog was squashed to death.

If I gets to find one, I thought, *I'll have it in the blue sugar bag before I lets on I got it.* That was the only way to keep it safe.

The first day left everyone happy with a job well started, but we were dirty and tired as we dragged all our bits back to camp.

As in the pea fields, the young boys would leave earlier in the evening

18. Furry yellow or green caterpillars of the Pale Tussock Moth.

to light the fires and ready the kettle for dinner on our return. The thought of frying tatters, eggs and bacon would have us all dropping our vines and scrambling back to the fire. Once there it was all go again; fires had to be lit, food cooked, and – worst of all – children had to be washed! One woman called out to us as me mam tried to scrub the smell of hops right out of our bones.

"You'll wash your lot away one of these days, my Vie!"

"You won't say that when you can't get the dirt out of your lot's necks and ears, Rody," me mam shot back, never letting up with the scrape of soap across my neck.

"A bit of dirt never killed nobody," laughed Rody, "and this dirt is clean dirt!"

Never mind the dirt – the comb pulling through my long wet hair nearly killed me. "Ow, Mam, let me do it!" I cried.

"No." She reached up with the comb. "You only combs the front, and you got a mat of tangles on the top of your head!"

It made me wish I never had any hair on me head at all, but to have it short was against the rules in those days. My hair was supposed to be my pride and joy, but right at that moment I couldn't have cared less about anyone's pride. When it was over I settled by the fire, eating and drinking as I listened to the grown-ups' banter.

"How many bushels we pick the day?" Old Joby asked me dad.

"Not enough, my Joe," he replied.

Joby nodded. "Each day it will get better. Though me hands is sore with they vines."

"Well, you know what you gotta do about that," me dad said seriously. "Take a walk down to the copse and run your own water over them. Let it soak in, then make sure you wash 'em good and clean."

"I ain't gonna piss over me own hands, is I now?" he laughed. "Good job I knows you're joking, Lenard!"

Me dad laughed before taking pity on Old Joby. "Salt water is the thing, an' bacon fat rubbed in after. It works a treat, as well you knows, old man."

"I'm off to do it now," he said.

In fact we all used the salt water and fat to harden up our hands against the vines. In a few days we would be able to pick through the day without any pain at all.

The warm fire and delicious smells would bring the town-pickers' children creeping after us, and no matter how many children were in each Traveller family, we would all welcome a number of town children to share our food and drink with us. We would usually keep the same children through the season, as if they were our own.

I don't know when this tradition first started, but even when me dad was a young boy he shared his food with the town-pickers. I don't remember their mothers ever asking us to feed their offspring, though on occasion one would drag her child away, growling at them about eating the 'Gyppos' food'. They were usually new to picking with us, but even those children soon found their way back to the fire. Those new pickers would soon be put right by the other townsfolk for, over the years, they had got to know us and grown used to our ways – and that involved making sure that no child would ever grow cold or go hungry if we could help it.

Besides, after being out in the fields for so long it seemed best to have a few mouthfuls of hot grub rather than just bread and cheese all day long.

With the weather kind and food in our bellies, the mood in the garden would change from a quiet place to a jolly one. One Traveller would start singing an old song to himself, and softly the old words would infect everyone – town-pickers and all – so in the dense garden other voices would join in the song, though you would not be able to see the singers, spread out as we were. Nothing could beat it – nothing could come near those songs sung amid the hops. We had sometimes heard choirs singing on the wireless on a Sunday afternoon, but I would bet my lot singing in the hop gardens were as fair a chorus as most of them. Every crabby-tempered Traveller turned into a song thrush.

The hop season was also a time for making deals, and across the singing and chatter we often heard the men discussing grys.

"That's a nice little tit[19] you got," I heard one man say.

"Yeah, she ain't for sale," said the owner, though we knew full well she was. It made for a better and longer deal, and the men all knew it. They would go through the breeding of the horse, chamming[20] on for what seemed like hours before we'd hear the smacking of hands that sealed the deal, loud in the garden. It was more entertainment and enjoyed by all.

You'd get young bits of boys and gals making sheep eyes at each other, trying hard not to be noticed – for a hop-vine round the chops is not so nice, if the parents caught on. Most families didn't want their children to be courting too early. They'd lose a worker if they had a runaway! Parents kept a strict eye on those that wanted to start courting and even if they were deemed old enough it would be a long old engagement. No family back then wanted a runaway on their hands before they were married. This is a strict part of Romani culture and any scandal was talked of for generations, giving the family a bad name.

There was another thing that could crop up in the hop-picking season, though not often by any means. I remember, on occasion, one of the gals or women from the big towns would come to talk with us, having got themselves in 'a bit of trouble' – that is, having a baby. Unable to take it back home with them, many things could happen to the baby – things that were never talked about. On the rare occasion, a Romani family would give the baby a home and a life with them. I know one man who has been in our family for the past sixty-odd years. He knows how he came to us, because his family told him as he grew up, but this is his way of life and he will always be a Traveller man.

---

19. A filly – a female horse under four or five years old.

20. Boasting about the horse's virtues in a kind of game.

Chapter Twelve

Lenard's Dilemma

ONE EVENING, ME DAD and his brothers – Jim, John and Jessie – were talking about the old granny and granddad. They had discovered that their sister Emily had run away with a man called Blacksmith Joe. Emily had been like a right arm for her parents, staying at home longer than most daughters would to look after the cooking and shopping and other duties. Now she looked to be going travelling and it left a gap the brothers would need to fill, for their sister would want to live her own life with her new man.

"They will dearly miss her," said Jim. "We'll have to chat with Blacksmith Joe. Perhaps he'll stay with me mam and dad."

"I bet you he don't," scoffed John. "How can a man earn his living by staying in the lane?"

"We'll all have to take our turns to stop with the old pair and let Emily travel off for a bit," Jessie said. "They two ain't getting any younger."

"Me dad ain't too good most of the time with his gout and legs. He can't fetch water or wood like he used to," added John.

From left to right: Aunt May, Blacksmith Joe, Little Lenny, Young Emmy, the old granny, dear old granddad and Kizzie. Down the Prince Lane, late 1950s.

"What's it to be, then?" asked me dad.

"We got no choice, have we?" answered Jim. "They looked after us, now it's our turn to do the same for they two. It'll be hard on our Lenard, mind, knowing how me mum treats Vie and the young 'uns."

"There is that to think of," answered me dad. "My Vie will answer back – she can't keep her gab shut, though me mum do ask for it."

"You'll just have to pull your wagon up the lane a-ways out of her reach," suggested John. "Besides, there's Tom and our Kizzie to think on. That poor bugger ain't gonna get any better with that bad complaint he got."

"Well, we'll just have to make the best of it then," said me dad. "I shan't leave 'em in the lurch, that's for sure. I'll do my share."

Oh dear, I thought. I just knew when he told me mam that sparks would fly. She would live a dog's life up at the Prince Lane, and I knew taking me and our Alfie up there would be the last thing she should want, but this too is part of our culture. The old and infirm would never be put in a home or neglected. It's up to the family to care for each other, no matter what – and although me mam believed this too, she wouldn't take it lying down.

If only the old granny had been different, for the thought of seeing more of me granddad and Tom was pleasing to us all.

That night, when they all went back to their wagons, me dad told me mam what the brothers had all decided.

"Now, don't fret, my Vie, but me and the rest been talking." Dad explained the situation with Emily and the blacksmith and how Tom's TB was growing worse. Mam gestured for him to get to the point. "Well, it's like this," he said. "Me and the others have decided to take turns spending more time with the old pair."

"Well, Lenard, you'll do it on your own then. I shan't put my children through too much of your old mother!"

"My Vie, what choice have I got, eh?" he argued, but me mam stayed firm.

"Let me tell you, Lenard," she said. "If you look over that hedge you'll see the road – and the man's long dead that made it. You can use it. Go back and stop with that old cow of a mother whenever you likes!"

"Let's drop it for now," me dad ordered. "There's time enough when the hops is over."

"Hops or no hops, I ain't living me life up that lane!"

"I loves you, my Vie, and you knows it, but there's things that must be done in this life!"

"Then you do it on your own!"

And so it went on for half the night, ending up with them at loggerheads with each other.

The next morning was Saturday, and so all the grown-ups dressed up like ham bones and got in their carts and trolleys ready to go to town for the shopping.

"Now, Maggie, you knows what I told you," warned me mam as she launched into the familiar list. "Keep the fire on, peel the tatters and mind the rest. No fighting, stay close to the wagon and no running off till I gets back. Did you hear me, Maggie?"

"Yes, Mam," I chirped. "Mind the rest of 'em, no fighting and stay by the wagon."

"Mind you do, or you'll get nothing when I gets back. You're a big gal now, so you do as you're told."

I will, I thought. *If that little mush Alfie leaves me alone.*

There were a few grown-up gals left behind on the field to keep an eye on us. They'd been tricked into it with a promise of being let out to the pictures that evening. Alfie and Robert fetched wood from the heap and filled the cans with water, before heating up some soapy water to wash down the wheels of our wagon. Then they went off with the boys across the field while I looked after my brother Jessie and baby Emily. Some of the big gals joined us and we chatted around the fire while waiting for the grown-ups to come back.

I left our Emily sleeping in the big pram near the fire while Little Jess curled up on me lap. He was missing me mam terribly.

"When's they coming back, then?" he asked over and over.

"Be a good boy and I'll make you a drink, eh?"

"Don't want no drink. I want me mam."

"Well you can't have her so shut up," I said, before soothing him. "She won't be long now."

Jessie was a mummy's boy. How he loved me mam! He hated it when she was out of his sight and I bet that, out of all of us left on the field, it was Little Jess that she worried over.

It was late afternoon afore the traps and trolleys started to roll through the gate and we were all excited to find out what the grown-ups had brought back for us. I hung onto Jess for dear life as the horses came up, trying to stop him from running beneath their feet as he caught sight of his mam. It was kushtie when they gave us each a pig's trotter and our fair share of sticky lardy cake, and, just when we thought that was all, me mam brought out a bag of tangy yellow sherbet each, as payment for our help picking the hops. We felt very lucky indeed!

As they fussed over us I thought that it looked as though me mam and dad had made up, but I had to wonder what it had cost him or what promises he had made to her.

That evening he got ready to go to the pub with his brothers and the other men. "How do I look, my Vie?"

"Same as you looked just now," she answered.

Me dad shook his head. "You ain't right in the head!"

"I can't be, for I ended up with you," she laughed. "But you mind what I said, now: no chopping[21] out our horses or me wagon. I know what you's like with the lush down your neck."

"I'll mind. Don't you worry so."

"I mean it, Lenard. Chop and deal as much as you like, but leave me wagon and horses alone. And no fighting, you'll get locked up."

"Is there anything I can do?" he asked.

"Yes," said me mam, "behave yourself! I knows what you and they brothers of yours is like when let loose." With that, me dad said his goodbyes to us all and left with his brothers for the evening.

The next day was Sunday and we had a fat roast chicken as a treat for our dinner. Me mam loved to make a roast each Sunday and she was good at it! The big black pot was pushed into the hot embers of the fire to heat up the fat and the tatters, onions and stuffed chicken were all put inside it, roasting nice and slow.

Me dad was off across the field, checking on the horses and gathering wood, so mam made us pancakes for tea and to take out on

---

21. selling; dealing

the garden the next day. We were all enjoying her cooking till the awful smell drifting over on the wind hit us.

Sheep's panch.

The panch is the gut of the sheep, cleaned with a scrubbing brush before being boiled over a fire. It stunk like a fox as it cooked and we could never stand it! We always begged our mam to never buy the panches for we couldn't force ourselves to eat it. It was a popular meal for most Travellers, though rarely on a Sunday.

In the evening the men went off rabbiting. Most families would be having rabbit stew out on the garden tomorrow, so we started getting everything ready for it. The stew would be very welcome in the cold garden, left to cook slowly on the fire so all the flavours were strong and warm. We liked to prepare our meals a day ahead, otherwise working on the fields we risked not having much. I helped me mam make some swimmers – dumplings with extra pepper – so that they were ready for when me dad got back with the rabbits.

It was his job to gut and skin the rabbits, though me mam was a fair hand at it. We saved the skin to be stretched and dried to sell at the rag stores later on. We never wasted anything if we could help it, always making sure there was some way to make a living. Though we knew we were secure in the hop gardens for a few more weeks at least, we had no guarantees after that and a long winter would soon be approaching. Who knew what surprises were in store?

As the weeks went by and the hop season drew slowly towards its end, we began to make our preparations for leaving the hop gardens.

The women had ordered their wares from the china shops of Ledbury and were paying the money over week by week. Me mam had bought a china punch bowl and we all thought she deserved it, for she had worked hard this year in the gardens.

It wasn't long before the men were due to pick up the fine suits of clothes they had ordered weeks before: jackets with fancy belts and pleats in the back, new trilby hats and a few caps and neckerchiefs. It would all be packed away till the first horse fair, when the men would dress up and show off in their finery as they chopped and dealt.

We were now picking in the last part of the garden, with only a few days before we would all have to say farewell to our friends and family and spread out once more down all roads. It was a sad time because we had grown fond of the other Travellers and town-pickers we had grown to know. At least we knew that their children would think of us fondly, with memories of our fry-ups and stews. They would never forget their introductions to the hop-dogs, even if we never met them again.

As each family set out, they would pick a bunch of the best hops to tie to the front of their wagon. This was a good luck charm which we all hoped would bring us success for the next hop season and we would let them hang until they fell apart. We would then drop them in a hedge so that any seed could take life. This way, our hops could grow over a wide area of the country, marking the paths we travelled.

As we readied to leave, our parents said their fond farewells to the townspeople they had come to know. Some of the mothers of the children we had helped look after were very grateful, calling our family kind-hearted and the like. It was nice to know we had touched their hearts, for not many house-dwellers got to spend weeks with us, getting to know our ways, and we are often painted in a bad light with folk.

The farmer was pleased with our work and booked us for the following year, shaking our hands in farewell. Me dad's brothers, heading to the Prince Lane, had pulled out a day before us, except for John and his wife Ellen, who planned to travel back with us for a while. We planned to stop around Keynsham for the winter, making up wooden flowers and pegs to hawk before Christmas, when we could start making holly wreaths. After that, we would head to the old granny and granddad, to give the rest of the family a chance to travel awhile.

The horses were fresh and eager to be off and as we headed back onto the road we could see trails of smoke from the Queenie stoves billowing out of other wagons, marking the paths of the Travellers ahead of us.

Chapter Thirteen

School Days

IT WAS COLD OUTSIDE as we travelled on towards Bristol, but we were kept warm inside the wagon while me dad walked ahead of his horses as he always did when they were rested and fresh. Once they had settled down he would hop up upon the foreboard of the wagon and guide them from there.

As we met the main road we saw the wagons turning off in all directions. Some came along with us, but we knew that we would lose them all in a scant few miles or so. It seemed like slow going, heading back towards our part of the country, but eventually we neared Bristol and then on past Keynsham to Corston, a little hamlet outside of Bath.

We pulled up in a lane off the main drag, settling under a railway bridge. Uncle John had caught a chill somewhere along the road and was not well at all, coughing and spluttering, but he would get better and things would soon get back to normal.

Not so for we children, for our mam had been busy while we travelled unaware, and now she broke the news to us: me and our Alfie were going to school and it was only a couple of days before we were due to start. We'd never been to school before and didn't want to. We played her up something awful, crying and carrying on, refusing to fetch wood or water. We tried every trick we knew to get her to change her mind.

"Why're you punishing us, Mam?" we groaned. "What have we done?"

"You're gonna learn to read and write," she told us.

"We don't want to read or write!"

"I'll never go to school!" cried Little Jess, clinging to his mam. "I won't, Mam!"

Robert carried on that he wanted to come to school too, but was told no. I'd bet he only asked because he knew me mam would never let him. She considered him too young to be left with strangers.

Me dad didn't want us to go either and dared to say so. "We shan't be here long enough for they two to learn nothing."

"They's going to school," she said. "If it's only for a few days, they's going."

What could we do with a mam like that? Come the dreaded Monday morning we were dragged to that school. I scraped my feet all the way to the gates and so did our Alfie. By the time we got there me mam was sweating and panting and all the other children were inside the brick building, ready for the day. As we went through the door I could see the whites of Alfie's eyes, his face pale and peaked, and I know mine must've been the same. We were both crying buckets by the time the teacher woman came to meet us.

"Please, Mam," we begged, sobbing all the while.

"Now stay with this nice lady," she told us.

"Please, Mam, please. We'll be good, just take us back!"

The teacher woman was a big old gal who smiled at me mam and promised to take care of us. She told me mam not to worry, but all eyes were on us two as she left us to the teacher and the school.

"Now shut this crying up, you two big babies," said the teacher as she pushed us both into a corner of the room. We noticed how she wiped her hands on her skirt, as if to wipe away some dirt, but me mam had bought us both a new rig-out, including shoes, and had washed us (as usual) to within an inch of our lives. The teacher shut the door to the room and Alfie and I looked at each other in fright. Never before had we two been in a room with the door closed, aside from shops, and we felt this were a bad situation to be in.

"Do you think me mam will come back?" I asked our Alfie.

"How do I know?" he sniffled, as the teacher barked at us to keep quiet. We carried on muttering till she turned to us sourly.

"Will you two Gypsies keep quiet? These children are here to learn, even if you're not!" She turned away as if we couldn't hear her. "What have I done to deserve Gyppos?"

What a nasty person she was. The longer we stayed in that room, the more I began to fear that our parents would move on without us and leave us behind. Eventually, I said so to Alfie.

"I'm thinking the same," he whispered back. "When that door opens we'll both run for our lives."

"You won't leave me, will you?"

"Not if you runs fast and keeps up with me."

"Please, my Alfie, don't leave me," I begged, not able to stop the tears that came. I suddenly found meself being shook like a rabbit in a dog's jaw. I'd never seen the teacher woman coming at us, but now she smacked me round the head.

"I warned you," she said, as Alfie cried out to defend me, getting a smack as well for his troubles. The class laughed as she told us we were nothing but dirty little Gypsies, and Alfie reared himself up.

"We ain't dirty!" he hollered. "You lot is dirty, and you stink!"

Time passed in that classroom until the teacher gave all the children a little bottle of milk each. All but us, but we wanted nothing off her. After they'd finished they were let outside to play for a while, but as we headed for the door she shut it on us.

"Not you two," she said, hand on the door. "Stay where you are – you're going nowhere." We could hear the children playing outside and thought that if we could only get out of this room we would run like the wind, back to the wagons and our family.

When they finally came back into the room, a ginger-headed boy came over to us, spat at and then punched our Alfie. Well, never knowing when to quit, our Alfie punched the boy back and all hell broke loose. It was a free-for-all as boys and gals rushed at us. We fought like tigers and though there were many of them we managed to leave our mark on a fair few – and they on us.

The teacher woman stood by the door, watching us carrying on but doing nothing to stop it. Another woman appeared, drawn by the shouting, and hollered to one and all to return to their desks. Everyone stood down meekly and the strange woman turned to the teacher and asked what was going on. The teacher replied that we two had attacked the others. We were wild animals, she said.

"When I came in here you were letting the whole class fight one another." The woman glared at the room in general. "There are only two of them, how on earth did you let it get so out of hand?"

"It was the Gypsies," the teacher said again. The stranger stood still for a moment before telling our teacher to go outside with her.

As soon as they were out of the room our Alfie turned to glare at the ginger-headed boy. "I'll give you a hiding the first chance I gets," he warned.

"Yeah?" he laughed and spat at us again.

"That's not a threat but a promise," said our Alfie, and the look on his face told the class they were for it. "And me sister'll fight you gals," he added.

I groaned quietly as we moved away. "But Alfie, look how many there is! They'll kill me stone dead."

"Well, fight harder," he hissed. "They won't come back if you get the first punch in. Sting the first one and the rest will run."

"I don't know, my Alfie, there's some big old gals over there."

The teacher woman came back into the classroom looking as though she could kill us both. How we wished we could've had that other lady. She looked strict, but not unfair.

It seemed like forever till finally lunchtime came along. As the children got ready to leave the room our Alfie turned and told me to get ready to run for me life. He said it in Romani Chib – our own language – so that none of the others would know what we had said. We usually spoke this language when we were together and it was so precious to us all. Back then we spoke very little plain English on a daily basis, though I'm writing these memoirs in it now.

As the door opened for lunch, Alfie gave a hard shove. We took off through the door to an uproar behind us – the other children were hollering and shouting as we ran. Alfie jumped gracefully over the gate, but I was grabbed roughly by one of the teachers as I was climbing up over it and that was the last I saw of him.

I was taken back to the classroom and pushed back into the corner as the teacher woman shut the door. I was on my own now and couldn't help but sob bitterly. After a while, the nice lady from before came in to talk to me. She was so different from my teacher, even trying to put her arms round me to comfort me as I cried. I was having none of it, though, convinced that I'd never see me family again.

"I want me brother," I cried as she tried to coax me into having some dinner. "I don't want any food! I wants me mam, me dad. I wants to be let out!"

The woman tried her best but I wouldn't listen. I felt sick by now, I had not been to the lavatory nor had any bread or water all day. I couldn't stop crying, even as the other children laughed.

Finally, I heard a commotion by the door and watched as the nice teacher led me mam into the classroom. Oh Gawd, me mam had come for me. Again, I cried bitterly.

"What's been going on with my two children?" she asked the two women.

"Nothing, Mrs Smith," replied the nasty teacher.

"Nothing!" me mam exclaimed. "Look at the state of my gal!"

I did look a sight, with scratches on me face and arms from the other children and red eyes swollen like a gurnet fish from me tears.

"She missed her brother," the teacher woman said.

Now me mam pushed out her chest. "I never sent my two to be beat by you, missus. If they wants beating, I'll be the one to do it, not you."

"I didn't beat your children, Mrs Smith," replied the teacher, but me mam saw the way she looked at me and I thought that she wouldn't have liked the teacher any less if she had been the one to lay hands on me.

"No, and it don't look like it," me mam scoffed. "I'll tell you something. If my two looks tomorrow like they do today, I'll be handing out a beating alright – and you'll be the one getting it."

"Take your little girl home now," said the nice teacher, turning to glare at the other woman. "This will not happen again, I promise you."

Oh, how I was glad to get out of that room. As we walked back to the wagons I clung to me mam, begging her not to send me back to that place again. "Oh, Mam, I ain't going back in there! They all hates me!"

"You'll go back on the morrow," she replied softly.

Me dad went mad when he saw me. "They ain't going to no more schools!" he hollered, but me mam stood firm.

"They will," she said.

"Then over my dead body!" he vowed.

The next morning we were dragged back to school and me father was still alive and well, swearing that we need not go. Things at the school weren't much different. We stayed quiet in the corner while the other children were villains. We were no better than they and for each sly punch we received we gave back another two and twice as hard. The teacher woman hated us, turning a blind eye when the boys were kicking or spitting or punching but always managing to notice when we two fought back.

At least that day we were given the little bottles of milk and a warm lunch, but if we wanted to lay down after it was on the floor and not on the mats that were given to other children. We weren't given any pencils or paper either, but that was no hardship, for we knew very little of what the teacher was on about.

A few days later the teacher began discussing foxes and badgers with the other children and we wondered how she could mean the animals that we knew. Me and our Alfie talked it over and realised that we knew more about wildlife than the woman did, which was so kushtie that it made us brave.

"Foxes don't act like that," Alfie would say and, "Badgers don't eat those."

"Mind your business and keep quiet," the teacher said. "If you listen you might learn something."

How we laughed at that. We could have told her the same.

Chapter Fourteen

The Squatters' Hut

THE WEEKS WENT BY and John's illness got no better. Eventually, the doctor came out to visit him and soon after another man came and told us they had a place with running water where we could go. Worried about John, me mam and Ellen agreed.

"I don't know so much," me dad said. "A squatters' hut on an old army camp? I just don't know, my Vie. First our two go to that school and now you wants us living in a squatters' hut."

"Give over, Len," me mam scoffed. "You're never game for nothing. Let's give it a try, eh?"

"Fine. Only if I don't like it we shift on."

We packed up to leave and head for the camp, me and our Alfie singing all the while, "No more school, no more school!" We were over the moon and as our wagon passed by the school we waved it goodbye. Mam didn't hear us, or we would've been quickly corrected.

After about two and half miles we pulled into the camp gates to see a man waiting for us and before we could say much at all we were allocated a squatters' hut. Me poor old dad looked about him and shook his head in dismay.

"What have I come to?" he asked himself.

"It's only till John is back on his feet," said me mam with a gleam in her eye that allowed no argument. "You knows he ain't well."

"Neither will I be, having to live here," dad replied.

The huts were big barn-like buildings with a tin roof, two bedrooms and a front room with a big wood-burning stove right in the middle of it. Ellen and John had the hut next door to us, so we were all together at least. The only one who took to that hut was me mam, who straight away set about sorting the beds and tables and chairs how she liked them. John didn't care overmuch, for he felt so ill.

As they were sorting themselves out, me and our Alfie stayed outside, looking around our new home. I felt a sudden whack on me arm as Alfie spotted something. I turned to look and could've dropped dead from surprise. There in our sights was that ginger-headed boy from the school, standing with his mates.

Alfie smiled in a way that promised mischief. "I'm gonna like this place," he told me. "Ain't you, Maggie?"

I looked at the shock on their faces as they spotted us and had to laugh. "Yeah, I'm gonna love it here."

We were stunned that they could be living here, same as us. They ran away suddenly, sprinting through the camp. We called out to Robert and Little Jess and took off after them, ignoring our mam calling us back. We were set on a fight, finally having the chance to get back at those boys for the weeks of torment. We'd been hit and spat on and now the culprits were right in our hands, outside of the school, and no teacher was around to stop them from getting back all they had dished out.

We found them in an old deserted hut, their eyes blazing something fierce. We pulled up short, knowing that they meant to beat us, but we four had been brought up rough and ready. Alfie threw the first punch and me and Robert strode fearlessly in after. We threw ourselves into the scrap, fighting viciously with the gang of boys. I was in me element for they never expected a gal like me to fight with them, but they soon realised I was ready to stick up for meself. It didn't take long for Little Jess to run back to me mam, scared of all the fighting, but by then we had the upper hand against the town boys.

The boys ran off and we knew we would be in trouble when me mam and dad found out, so we headed back to our hut like three little sheep.

"You've been fighting," accused me dad.

"No we ain't!" I said. Me plaits were hanging loose and there was blood on Alfie's nose but I swore our innocence. Before he could get the story out of us a gang of men and women came galloping over, shouting and swearing.

"Your bloody bastards have beaten up my boy," shouted one big mush.

"Oh, have they then?" asked me dad.

"Yeah they have! We don't want you Gypsies staying on this camp, so pack up and get going!"

"And you're the man who's going to make us, is you?" me dad said, straightening up.

"I don't want any thieving Gyppos living here," said the man.

"Hang on, my Len." Me mam looked me dad in the eye. "Don't you get fighting, we've only just got here." No sooner had she said that than the women started shouting at her, screaming about their children and how we had hit them. Me mam puffed out her chest and told the women how we'd been treated at that school.

"My children have done nothing to yours," said one woman.

"Right. Alfie, Maggie, come here," ordered me mam. We didn't dare disobey. She pointed at the woman who'd spoke. "And now you, missus, you fetch your lot here and we'll soon sort this out."

"And I'll knock your bloody heads off," hollered me dad, "coming over here, calling me and mine names!"

I turned to Alfie with tears in me eyes. "Oh, Alfie, what've we done?"

"Shut your gab and stop crying," he scolded me. "You ain't no baby."

Soon about nine children were fetched to our hut, though not all of them had been in the fight. Me mam ordered us to tell the truth about what we'd gone through at the school, but they said we were telling lies. Their families stayed loyal to them and got noisy about it until one little gal spoke up.

"They have too been doing it," she said. "Everyone knows and joins in, hitting them in school and in the playground. You can ask Miss."

"The teacher?" asked one mum.

"Yes, she'll tell you."

The parents turned on them then, the big mush glaring down at his boy like thunder. "What have you lot got to say for yourselves, then?"

"We don't like them," said the ginger boy. "We don't want them dirty Gypsies in our school."

His father went to hit him but me dad called for him to wait. "Alfie, come here and get your shirt off," said me dad.

"What are you doing now?" asked the mush.

"Your boy wants to fight my boy, but they can't fight fair in that school. Let them fight fairly here, we'll be the judge of it, and afterwards you and me can get at it, mister, and I'll show you what a 'Gypsy man' can do."

I was very proud of my brother. He seemed much smaller than the other boy but he took his shirt off and stood fearlessly, like a grown man. "Come on then," he said, squaring up to the bigger boy. The boy ran off, refusing to fight.

"You and me then," said me dad, ripping his shirt off and squaring his shoulders.

"I'm sorry," said the boy's father. "I won't fight, but I will give that boy a beating he won't forget in a hurry. I'll be at the school on Monday morning and I'll speak to those two teachers."

"Mister," warned me mam, "I didn't born and bring up my children to be kicked and punched by the likes of you lot and I'll stand for no more of it. Every day I've had to drag these two to that school, and all because of your bastards."

"It won't happen again," they said. "I'll promise you both."

After everyone had left, me dad threatening to make the whole camp ring if we returned with another mark on us, our parents argued for a while whether we should pack up and leave as soon as possible.

"I shan't let the likes of they people drive me out, Len," said me mam. Bless her, she really wanted to stay in her hut, but me dad couldn't see it. He finally agreed, but we knew we hadn't had a good start in that place.

Alfie was strutting around like a fighting cock, saying the big boy was frit to take him on. I really do think he found his confidence that day. He'd never been afraid of much, but having me dad's full back-up for his decision to stand up for himself made a real difference. He felt like a man.

After that, life at the school changed for the better. We still stayed in the corner but were left alone to chatter to each other and never took any notice of the lessons. We did pick up the words of the chanting and singing that the children did every day, our enjoyment of songs and rhymes peeking through, and we learned all the times tables by rote before we even realised it.

Me dad had still not taken to the squatters' hut, and as the weeks went by he grew more and more unhappy staying in one place. In fact, me mam was the only one of us who liked it, for she had running water and a place to call her own. We were glad when ragging time came round as it gave me dad and John the chance to get out into all the nearby towns and villages.

During ragging time we would buy all manner of things from the house-dwellers to make use of or sell on elsewhere. Me dad and John would go out on a trolley they had bought, dropping rag-bills advertising for rags and woollens we could re-sell, as well as for bones, rabbit-skins and all manner of metals – iron, brass, copper, zinc, aluminium and gun-metal – for they sold well in the towns.

Despite school, we would still go out with dad to drop the rag-bills through the house-dwellers' doors, singing the rhyme that made up our advertisement. We didn't know who had made up the rhyme for us, but many Traveller families had copies and variations of it. We had them printed in many colours – pink, yellow, red, blue and green – as we lost many of the bills once they had been pushed through the doors.

Our rag-bill read:

50 TONS OF RAGS WANTED
We Will Call Back In Two Hours

The above, with most respectful feeling,
Begs to inform you what he deals in.
He's not come your purse to try,
Yourself shall sell, and he to buy.

I buy old stockings,
Trousers, vest and jackets,
So please look up your useless lumber
Which long may you have left to slumber.

Dusty rags, sacking and old bags,
Car batteries, pewter and old brass,
Old stew pans, boilers and copper kettles,
Pewter spoons and other metals,

I buy old iron, cast or wrought,
And pay the money when it's bought,
So over your dwelling give a glance,
You'll never have a better chance.

My price is good, my weight is just
And, more, I never ask for trust.
So please look up an extra handful
And for the same I will be thankful.

However small your stock, I'll have it.
Please return this circular when called for.
Thank you.

We were often asked by house-dwellers where the rhyme came from, but it had been in our hands for so long that where it had come from was lost. One tale was that a Romani man had made it up and a house-dweller had written it down into English from the Romani's own chib. This sounded reasonable to me, for I had grown up with the rhymes and songs made up by Travellers and knew we had that creativity in us.

We collected all that the house-dwellers sold us in rag-bags. Sorting the rag-bags was always exciting for us children because we could find all manner of things we could use, such as toys and clothes and the like. I always checked the pockets of the clothes we had been sold and would often find money, pocket knives, watches and jewellery that hadn't been cleaned out. My crafty old dad would take it from me, though, thanking me for looking through the pockets for him, and like a dope I would fall for it every time.

Each year me mam would holler at us to keep out of the rag-bags, saying we'd be lousy with nits and fleas and then we'd know it. "Lenard," she would sigh, "talks to these children, for Gawd's sake."

Me dad would holler at us for me mam's benefit, "Get out of they rag-bags, you lot, I shan't tell you again!" before leaning in to whisper to me, "Have you found anything good, Maggie?"

"Shan't tell you," I would sing. "You just hollered at me."

"Come on, my baby, tell your old dad what you found."

"Only a shet-knife[22], dad," I'd say back, knowing he'd be pleased.

Me dad loved the old shet-knives that flicked open and closed. He had dozens and would give them as presents to other Traveller men whom he had a deep feeling for. Many men and women did this with

---

22. pocket knife

small trinkets like knives and jewellery and I knew some men who kept me dad's gift with them for the rest of their lives and would take it to their graves as a charm for the friendship they'd had in life.

Chapter Fifteen

On the Road Again

LIFE HAD BECOME PEACEFUL on that old army camp. One day me and our Alfie finished our long walk from school to the camp to find that there was more family pulled on and in huts: me dad's brother Alfie and his family, Jim and May, so now our children well-outnumbered the others and we had a few more to walk to school with, for word had spread that we had found a place to stop that was out of arm's reach of the policemen. So it came as no surprise one day to find we had even more Travellers on site. This time it was John and Carrie Ayres and their family.

The families got on really well and we had even more company at school. We were overcrowded in our little spot now as we sat on the floor. One day a mush from the school board walked into the room and we overheard a lot of talk between him and the teacher about our being Traveller children. Days later, we were given hooks for our coats and pencils to draw with and the old caretaker brought in desks and chairs for us to sit on.

Much to the disgust of our teacher, the Traveller children came out of their little corner.

Making holly wreaths, Pedwell Hill, Ashcott, 1992. Me, mam and Robert.

As Christmas drew near me dad grew more and more restless. We carried on as we normally would – cutting holly for me mam to make wreaths and gathering mistletoe to sell in little bunches. There was a cooker in the huts, but the Traveller women decided to cook Christmas dinner outside as normal, saying that it wouldn't taste the same cooked inside the old hut.

That year we had a lovely Christmas. We hung our socks outside so as not to be missed by old Father Christmas, who might not think to look for us inside that Nissen hut. It really was a grand time for us, but as much as me dad enjoyed his time with the rest of us he had made up his mind that it was time to be moving on.

Me mam insisted that the squatters' hut was scrubbed clean before we left it – if she had to give it up, then she would do so in style and leave it shining and gleaming clean – not that she didn't already keep it spotless. She was sad that we were leaving, but me dad was determined to get back on the road.

"Hold your head up, my Vie. You know I stuck it as long as I could," me dad told her.

"I know, Len, but me children was getting educated and it was good to be in one place for a bit."

"My Vie, you know our two have never learned a thing in that school except how to be cheeky," me dad said. "The first day we shifted up here it was bedlam."

With our horses hitched up we were ready for the off – no more school, just open roads ahead of us. We were travelling on our own and so exchanged many long farewells and promises to meet up again soon with John and Jim and their families as we pulled away.

"You're happy as a pig in a poke, ain't you?" me mam asked me dad with a hint of a sulk. We lot kept our thoughts about that to ourselves, trying to spare her feelings. We felt free for the first time in months even though we knew she would put us back into school wherever we shifted to next.

We travelled around for weeks, selling our wares and calling in the villages we passed. We were heading slowly towards the Prince Lane. Come the spring, Ticker would have her foal and me dad decided that the Lane would be the best place to take her. It also meant he could take his turn looking after me granddad and the old granny.

One afternoon we pulled into a quiet little lane near Bath and lit the fire ready for the cold evening. We hoped to stay there for a few days before moving on to the Prince Lane, but no sooner had we settled in than a policeman approached us on his pushbike. He greeted me mam and dad friendly enough and stood by the fire talking to them, while unbeknownst to him four pairs of yocks were glued to his pushbike where it he had dropped it by the bank.

"I could ride that pushbike," said our Alfie.

"So could I," Robert piped up, little Jess nodding his agreement.

I glared at them both. "What about me?"

"You're only a gal, our Maggie, and that's a man's bike," Alfie told me.

Still bickering quietly, we crept up to the pushbike and wheeled it up the road without being spotted. My, it was a big bike. We could hardly hold it upright, it was so heavy – but that didn't put off our Alfie. He was too small to reach the ground from the seat, so he lodged his feet under the cross bar as Robert, Jess and I held the bike up and gave it a push down the road. That bike must've had a mind of its own, for as Alfie fell the pushbike followed after him.

The crash and Alfie's hollering (he swore he'd kill us if we'd made him fall on purpose) brought me parents and the policeman running towards us. The policeman checked over his bike while me dad yelled at us for stealing and mucking about. Luckily for us, the policeman was a nice man, for he turned to me dad with a smile.

"Kids will be kids," he said.

"Mine knows better," replied me dad. "I'm sorry sir. You been so good as to give us a few days to stop here and look what my lot have done!"

Me dad was right. We did know better than to interfere with a policeman's runner. I don't know what had come over us – we'd be for it now and worst of all we'd never even got to have a ride! As we children hid behind the wagon the policeman took his leave. We knew we had done a big wrong and we were lucky that our mam stopped dad from laying into us. Instead, we were sent to bed without any tea – for me mam had been making a broth that we'd been looking forward to – and we were so hungry that we almost wished she'd never stopped me dad from going mad at us.

It was a lesson we never forgot. For the next few days we did every job we were asked to do and more without a squeak of complaint.

Spring that year already looked to be a warm one and the day we pulled out of that lane the sky was clear and bright. It was only a few weeks now until Ticker would have her new foal and she was fat as a pig. Me dad was hoping for a filly for breeding, but if it was a colt he knew he would sell it well at the horse fairs. He wanted to get to the Prince Lane as soon as possible, for there are Romani customs for when a mare foals down that we always obeyed.

Ticker had to be taken well out of sight of any women and children and be in a place where plenty of blackthorn grows. The foal would be born in a bag (or membrane), which would later be rolled up and placed in the blackthorn bush as a good luck charm for the mare and foal. The Prince Lane was full of blackthorn hedges and had a bend in the lane just out of sight of the wagons, where many foals had been born over the years.

Knowing we had Ticker's newborn to look forward to softened the dread we felt as we got nearer to the old Granny, but if we'd known then what was to come we would not have been so hopeful.

Chapter Sixteen

Death in the Family

I N THE WINTER the Prince Lane is a barren place but it was beautiful in the springtime, with wild flowers just peeping through the banks and catkins hanging on the nut hazels. How we enjoyed the spring of the year, yet still we pulled in with heavy feet.

As we pulled in we saw many other wagons pulled up around the lane. Most of me dad's brothers were gathered round, as well as me dad's other sister Jane, who was always called Touwie. She was a real villain, old Touwie and didn't like me mam one bit. Between her and the old granny we knew we'd be in for a rough ride, and because mam was not afraid of them, it made it worse. I always thought Touwie looked like a great black rook – even her head scarf was jet black atop her hair.

Me mam was pleasantly surprised to find that me dad's sister Emily and her new husband, Blacksmith Joe, were pulled up in the lane close to the old couple. We had all thought they were still off travelling. Mam was so pleased to see her, as she and Emily got on well. At least she would have one friend amongst them, I thought.

Most came out to welcome us as we came by and there were smiles and greetings all round – but the old granny stood back with a face on her as if to say, what do they want?

"Len, pull onto Johnny Ayres' piece[23]," me mam told me dad. "I'll not pull on the old woman's, I can see from here that she don't want us."

"Oh Vie, we ain't even unhitched yet and you're at it," me dad said, but he pulled up on Johnny Ayres' piece all the same. The land was owned by two families – granny and granddad and Johnny Ayres. We knew the Ayres well and knew that Johnny would let us have our own fire, whereas sharing with the old granny and Touwie would mean they would have more opportunity to throw a skit[24] over me mam. So for the sake of keeping the peace me dad did as he was asked, knowing that it would help keep me and our Alfie out of sight of his mam.

When we were unhitched and settled in, I was sent off with Alfie and Robert to fetch wood and water while the grown-ups greeted each other and exchanged any news. We soon had a good fire going and granddad wandered over for a sit down and a chat.

"It's kushtie to see you all. You children have grown like weeds," he said to us. "Come over and give your old granddad a kiss, I misses you when I can't see you."

We flew to his side, telling him we'd missed him too and we laughed together as he told us all that had been happening in our time away.

We had only been in the lane a few days when me mam began to seem worried. It wasn't over the old granny or Touwie, but something she wouldn't talk about.

"What's up, my Vie?" me dad asked her many times.

"Nothing."

---

23. plot of land

24. insult; humiliate

"There's something on your mind," he said. "Has our Touwie been at you?"

"No, she knows better," me mam smiled. "We'll talk tonight when we're on our own," she promised him.

I stayed up late as I could, trying to hear some of that talk. I knew it was to do with Emily and Blacksmith Joe and I strained to catch their whispering.

"Emmy's expecting to go to bed," said me mam. This meant she was expecting a baby. She had told me mam that she would die, but her baby would live.

"You're off your heads, the pair of you," answered me dad.

"I'm only telling you what she told me!" she said and he mumbled something back at her. "Well, our Emmy believes it and nothing we can say will alter that."

On the morrow the brothers sat around our fire discussing the news me mam had shared with me dad. The bit of happiness that had been in the air was dashed as the news sank in – their sister believed she would die.

"Call Blacksmith Joe here," said Jessie. "Let's see what he's got to say for himself."

It was bad news when he reached the fire. "My Emmy believes it," he confirmed. "She will die having this child."

"How can that fool of a sister know what'll happen in six months' time?" demanded John. "You lot is barmy and wants putting away for listening to that rubbish."

On and on it went, while round the old granny's fire another meeting was going on between the women and Emily. We listened from a distance, fetching wood and water to keep out of the way as we tried to keep up with all that was going on. For days they swung from believing and disbelieving Emily, but she was so convinced that me mam sided with her in the end.

"If it's true I'll eat me hat!" announced me dad. "I've never heard nothing like it!"

"Time will tell," said mam sadly.

"You're as bad as our Emmy," he yelled. "All we gets out of her is 'wait and see, wait and see'."

"What is we to do then, Len? She believes it and there are things to be done."

He was quiet for a time before he answered her. "I'll talk to the rest come morning."

Back then, it was custom for us when someone was ill and dying, to return to all the old stopping places that had meant something to that person. We would take them back over their years, take them to where they had considered home. We knew we had a lot of travelling to do.

This was something new to us children, for we had not yet come across this old tradition. Before we had been born me dad had lost both a baby brother and a sister and we knew how much it affected him still. Alice had been fourteen when her frock had caught alight from their own fire. She had died from her burns. His eyes would mist up when he spoke of her. She'd been a pretty young girl and in so much pain when she'd died. On the other hand, poor little Ikie had never had a chance in life. He'd only been a baby when the old granny had taken him into her bed and rolled over him in the night.

Now it was Emily's turn, if we were to believe her, and she had many places she wished to visit before it was too late. The family was falling over itself to make her happy and do her bidding, making sure that if what she said was true, they could let her go with peace in their hearts and no regrets, for they would have fulfilled her wishes to the last.

Granddad was cut down with grief for he was so close to his daughter Emily, but he made up his mind that his wagon would be out on the road in line with the rest. We arranged for one of the young boys to drive it, as he would not be able to hold the reins in his poor old hands.

We could not travel for a couple of weeks yet, for Ticker had given birth to a filly which at any other time would've had me dad whooping with glee, for to have a coloured filly was grand indeed. His excitement was lost in the sadness of the family and though he often wandered up the lane to be near the horses, it was just his way of being alone to digest the family predicament. It was head-spinning to be so convinced that we would lose a healthy, robust family member.

John decided that he would stay behind with us to help look after the mare and her newborn and then we would all follow the rest together.

It was quiet and lonely down the lane once everyone else had pulled out. John pulled his wagon over near ours to share our fire and company. They would spend long hours going over what had befallen Emily for the weeks that we were in the Prince Lane.

The new foal was three weeks old when we decided it was safe for her to travel with us. Me dad placed her safely in a bag up to her neck and heaved her up onto the tailboard of John's trolley, so that the mare could be tied behind with her. This was the only way the young foal could travel until her hooves hardened up.

Though it took weeks for us to catch up with the family, many other Travellers had heard of our troubles and set out to join us and we picked up much company along the way. Strangers and old friends would travel with us for a couple of days before leaving again once others could take their place supporting us. We were grateful for their comfort and respect – gathering together in illness and death is a special part of Romani culture.

Once we caught up with the family we found that life was very much the same as it had always been. We went out calling each day with our baskets of pegs and flowers and Emily came along happily, not seeming ill at all as her baby grew inside her. Many of the women begged lovely clean baby clothes for her, but she would not accept them.

Me mam walked alongside Emily whenever we went calling. One day she turned to her with a careful look. "Look at me, Emmy," she said. "I'm half your size and I've had four children. What makes you think you can't have one?"

"I told you, little 'un," she said. She always called me mam 'little 'un'. "I shan't see this baby. It will be the death of me."

"You're just being silly," laughed me mam, but I knew she believed Emily's prediction.

"Tell that to my dead body when the time comes," Emily laughed.

Through a long, hot summer we travelled to Witney near Oxford, where Emily had bought her nice blankets over the years, and then on to Swindon. We journeyed all over Wiltshire, Bristol and Somerset and visited every stopping place Emily could think of.

In the beginning of October 1948 she took a bad turn and it was decided that we would take Emily on to Chapel Plaister near Box in Wiltshire where we could call a doctor and district nurse. Emily had been so bonny in health through the summer that the last doctor we had seen – Doctor Williams in Peasedown St John – had scoffed and shook his head when told of Emily's plight, calling us a very silly lot of people. Now we began to panic.

We pulled up on the common with many other Travelling families, all giving us space but remaining within shouting distance in case they were needed. Wood was piled up and we children went down to the little stream to play a while and bring back water.

A nurse soon came on her pushbike and stayed a long while with Emily at the wagon. She announced that Emily was having the baby and fled to fetch the doctor. Me mam stayed with Emily in the wagon, teasing and coaxing her along.

"Come on, my gal, let's show 'em how it's done. Let's have this baby afore the doctor gets here!"

"I can't have it, Vie, I tells you!" she sobbed.

The doctor came up to the camp on a horse and after a fair time with Emily told us that all would be well, but hours later the nurse sent for him again. When he went into the wagon for the second time he decided that Emily would have to go to hospital and our relief quickly turned to dread.

Our heads all bowed in frantic prayer but the ambulance took a long time coming. Still me mam was glued to Emily's side and as they brought her out the wagon she was calling for me mam.

"Come along with me, little 'un!" She cried it so hard that the ambulance men scrambled to make room for me mam in the back of their truck before taking them both away.

It took seconds for the men to hitch up their traps and trolleys, following the ambulance to the big army hospital that Emily had been taken to. We bewildered children were left behind, comforted by the other Traveller women who had not been close enough to the family to warrant going along with the others.

It seemed like years before we had any news, though it was really only a few short hours before the traps and trolleys travelled back with a lovely baby girl. They had needed to operate to get the baby. Our Emmy had never come round.

Devastation hit all on the common, struck dumb by the thought of Emily's own prediction months ago. Poor old granddad went out like a light as he was helped down off a trolley and it took a long time to bring him back round. It was unbelievable that his daughter's words had come so true. We all asked the same desperate questions – did we do enough? Did we help all we could? Did we make her happy?

The doctor came back to speak to our family the next day and we young ones were sent off to fetch wood and water. Whatever they were told confirmed Emily's prediction. She would never have born a child.

Chapter Seventeen

Saying Farewell

THE DAYS LEADING UP to Emily's funeral were sad. It was decided that her child – named Emily for her mother – would be put into the loving care of Jessie and Louie, as Blacksmith Joe could not cope with bringing his daughter up alone. Jessie and Louie had big gals to help with the baby and enough money that they could afford the extra little one.

We had not slept for days during the sitting-up time, as is our custom, staying protectively nearby her body where it lay in the wagon, remembering all the times we had shared. Anyone who wanted to could say their own farewell to her and all night long grown-ups went up and down the wagon steps to pay their respects. The night before her funeral, at midnight, Blacksmith Joe went up into the wagon to say his final farewell to the woman who was his mate, wife and pal. They had been together for so short a time.

On the morning of the funeral Emily's coffin was brought out and laid on trestles. The lid was removed and we children were lifted up to kiss her face and say our goodbyes. They say that if you touch a body

Emmy's funeral at Paulton cemetery. This is all me dad's family, with mam in the front row with her handbag and Dad two to her right.

it will not play on your mind, so we smoothed her hair and touched her face to pay our own respects.

The funeral day dawned, clear and crispy cold. A charabanc had been ordered to carry the mourners and many other black cars were needed for all the family and a line of other cars and lorries followed their sad journey. Flowers spilled off the tops of cars and young Romani men drove the lorries that carried the rest of the ornate wreaths.

It was a long day for us left on the common, waiting and watching for our parents to get back to us. Emmy would be taken back to the family cemetery at Paulton, a few miles from the Prince Lane. Once they returned we waited together for nightfall. As the sun dipped Blacksmith Joe set light to the wagon that he and his wife had shared and we watched as their beautiful home burned to the ground. The night afore, Emily's brothers had cleared the wagon of anything that would not turn to ashes and had buried it deep in a secret place. I called these places our 'secret graves', where our china, brass, copper, candlesticks and other precious things were hidden away.

There the wagon burned, flames shooting up to the sky as hundreds of our family and friends watched on. The tears rolled down their faces as poor old granddad cried out for the good Lord to take him out of his misery. We were filled with such pain and grief.

The next morning Alfie, Robert and I were poking in the ashes of the wagon. We found silver sixpences and threepenny bits, money that Emily had been saving but that had been missed when her brothers had cleared the wagon. The coins were taken off us and passed around as keepsakes. I'm sure some of her grandchildren still have those same coins.

When all was finished, we headed back to the lane to spend some time with the old folks. The old granny was very quarrelsome, even more so than before, and poor old granddad was in the firing line.

Over the next few days the common slowly cleared. The old granny and granddad had been taken back to the lane and went as soon as they could to visit Emily's grave. They went most days. Blacksmith Joe found himself a pushbike and rode off the common with nothing but tears and the clothes he was wearing. Years later he married a gal called Betsy and they had a lovely family together.

Me dad had soon had enough and decided that it was time for us to move on. It was good to get away and lead our own lives again. We had Christmas at Emborough Ponds close by Chilcompton, near Radstock, but it was not a joyful time. Everywhere we went reminded us of Emily, and me mam and dad both felt her loss keenly.

We moved around the pea fields, picking one and then travelling on to another throughout the season, and then hung around Bridgwater till the fair. Me dad's mood lightened up at the fair – in fact he got as drunk as a handcart and was brought back to us in a trolley, singing his heart out for the first time in months. Me mam let him have it out and sing raucously and we knew she was as relieved as we were to see him

Blacksmith Joe and his second wife, Betsy, about 1955.

so merry. Any other time she would have split his head open to see him lushed up, for she hated to see him drunk.

The next day we pulled out in the hard, cold rain. We had decided to buy an old trolley and do a bit of ragging around Trowbridge through the winter. As we were on our own the ragging time would be a job for the whole family this year. Once we had bought the trolley we hitched Ticker up to it, letting her foul – Storm, we had named her – run alongside. Alfie or meself would drive the trolley along, bickering over whose turn it was to ride inside the wagon or guide old Ticker along. Storm was skewbald like her mother, and good and quiet to catch and tie up.

Winters could be very cruel. The wind and rain could blow the wagons over some years and it was hard to find hay for the horses. We usually tried to get field work, such as stone-walling, hedge-laying or logging, on the farms we knew. We often had to go out calling for food, trudging two or three miles to a village and thinking of the warm haven of our wagon and the fire waiting for us, only to find the lane bare when we returned and the old clumps of grass marking the way where the police had moved us along.

As winter turned once more to spring it was time to start picking flowers. We picked the snowdrops as usual but had to avoid the daffies, because they had to be picked on the sly. If caught, even me dad would be locked up and fined for trespassing, for the damage done by those strange Travellers had not been forgotten – or forgiven. How I loved the world in springtime. Every year I would wait for the sight of the little yellow celandine poking shyly out of a bank or verge. Once they bloomed all else would follow and no matter what the winter threw at them those little yellow flowers would always peep out to welcome the new season.

One morning in May, me dad announced that we were going back to the Prince Lane. "I'm worried about me dad," he said. "I needs to see if he's alright."

"I keeps getting him on me mind too," me mam answered, and you could see the relief in me dad's face at that. "Right, let's head our way back."

Spring was in full bloom as we travelled on the road. May blossom packed the hedges and their heavy perfume followed us along. Primroses and violets brought up the rear and seemed to smile as we slowly eased past. This was our world – the only one we knew. Open road and hedges in full bloom. We could watch the badgers at play and hear the birds singing as they made their nests and waited for their young to hatch. Foxes would bark to a mate and turn from lean animals to great fat ones as the rabbits and pheasants had their first litters.

We soon came across me uncle Tom's son, Pepper and his wife Amy. They had a young family and we were very fond of them all. Pepper was tall and a good worker and Amy was a dark and beautiful young woman who got on well with me mam. We were a contented little group on the lanes as the men dropped the rag-bills and collected them each day.

We weighed in at the big towns as we made our way to the Prince Lane. Granddad was very pleased to see us, but the old granny threw a few skits about us not worrying about them. This was daft since we had come so very many miles to visit and she had most of her sons already dancing to her needs. She wanted for nothing, yet Touwie was puffed up like a toad as she rounded on me dad.

"Oh, you managed to get back then," she cried. "No thought for the rest of us, stuck here and not earning enough to keep body and soul together!"

"Well, our old Touwie, you could've left any time. There's plenty here to look after me mum and dad. Nobody forced you to stay so keep that gab of yours shut!"

"Afore I do I'll tell you this, our Lenard: you're a skuss of bad luck[25] and no good will come of you!"

Me mam was furious at this. "If I do get a hit at you, Touwie, you won't want to travel. You'll be laying down for a month!"

"My Vie, ignore the nasty old bitch," spat me dad. "She was born wrong."

The rest of the brothers were glad to see Pepper and me dad and shook hands all round. We never stayed long though, for the rest were happy to stay with the old couple and me dad was satisfied that granddad was well cared for. Pepper decided to leave with us and so we travelled right up to Oxford, selling wooden flowers and wax roses, before moving on to Chapel Plaister.

---

25. Someone with the power to curse or bring bad luck.

Chapter Eighteen

Little Jess

CHAPEL PLAISTER WAS WELL KNOWN to us and so we knew many of the families that stopped there throughout the year. We children always had a grand old time on the common.

Standing at the gateway to the big house nearby was a big conker tree, with large, springy branches that could nearly touch the ground. We would sit or swing on them, letting them take us up and down in the air. We spent many happy hours on them old branches as children, laughing and squealing – and crying when we fell off. We got into so much trouble our fathers would regularly threaten to chop the old tree down, but thank goodness they never did!

Across the main road from our side of the common was a little bit of land owned by a gorgie mush named Mr Smith. He had a big shed on the land and sold fruit and veg around the villages off a horse and trolley. Over the years he had become a good friend to some of the Travellers who stopped on the common, not least me dad. We were also friendly with a woman in Box village who owned a teashop and knew each of us children by name, sneaking us little treats when we were in the village, calling.

We had been on the common for a few weeks, the men dropping rag-bills each day and weighing them in at the villages. One morning, the men decided they had collected enough for a weigh-in and borrowed Mr Smith's fruit trolley. It was packed high with the rag-bags.

That morning, me dad had promised to take Little Jess out with him – we others didn't know, for it was a real treat to go out with me dad on the trolleys and he knew it would have us fighting if he chose Jessie over us. Me mam kept us busy while Little Jess hid under the seat of the trolley. Pepper's big chestnut mare was hitched up to it. The horse was a gentle thing with one eye, big and strong enough to pull Pepper's heavy wagon on its own.

Later, we were told that when they were out of sight of the common, Little Jess came out from under the seat, laughing with glee that he had fooled the rest of us. He was placed between me dad and Pepper for his own safety. Not far up the road, Jessie spotted a two-shilling bit. Me dad jumped down to pick it up, giving it to Jessie, who laughed and promised to buy some hot tea and cakes with it.

They had reached the top of the hill that led to Chippenham when the horse shied and reared up so sudden that me dad fell off the trolley. The horse raced down the hill, me dad running after it, screaming at Pepper to save his boy. Pepper was fighting the reins to pull the horse up, but to no avail. A car came up behind me dad and, seeing his distress, the driver picked him up and hurried after the runaway horse.

Suddenly, Little Jess toppled off the trolley and fell under the wheel. Me dad leapt from the car, racing to his boy, who got shakily to his hands and knees. Both of the men sagged in relief as me dad gathered Jessie in his arms.

"Don't squeeze me, Dad," he asked and me dad held him gently as the man drove them quickly to the hospital.

Back on the common me mam had been on tenterhooks all day. A little white rabbit had come up to the wagons and no matter how many times we fetched it back up the road, away from our dogs, it hopped back up to us and would not leave.

"Amy, I don't like this happening," me mam said. "This rabbit is a skuss of bad luck. What do you make of it?"

"I don't like it no more than you do, my Vie," she admitted, worrying us all.

I remember that me mam was on her knees at the washing tub when a black car pulled up. Me dad came out of it, crying fit to burst. He was on his own.

Me mam took one look at him and let out a dreadful scream. "Where's me baby, Lenard? Where is he?"

Me dad could not speak. The taxi driver explained to me mam – they had come from the hospital – Little Jess was dead. He put me parents back into the car and took them to the hospital to be with our brother. We three bigger ones just stared at each other.

"What's happened?" Alfie asked me.

"I don't know," I said. "Our Jess – that man said he was dead."

We searched for Amy, needing answers, and found her crying hard up in her wagon.

"What's happened?" we cried.

"Your little brother is gone," she sobbed, wiping her eyes again and again. She could not see us for tears.

"What do you mean, he's gone?" our Alfie screamed. "Where's me brother? Where's he gone to?"

She just looked at us, her eyes red and wet, and we knew our Little Jess would never come home.

I can't remember much of the next couple of hours. We three clung to each other, crying our hearts out, for we were now old enough to know what death was. Alfie was eleven, I was nine, Robert was five and Emily about three. Little Jess had been seven.

When the black car brought me parents back our brother was still not with them. Me mam was carried out of the car, unable to raise herself. It was awful to see her arms and legs flopping about as they carried her up to the wagon – for a long moment we thought she too was dead. In a short time, the doctor and a policeman came to see us; Pepper and some other Travellers followed not far behind them.

That day was a blur to me. We stayed up round the fire all night and listened to me mam crying and me dad sobbing. Wagons, traps and trolleys soon began to pour onto the common to be with us – relations and friends from miles around. They had heard through the police what had happened. They had sent word to other police stations to tell the Travellers in their areas to spread news of our tragedy so we would not be alone and still me mam cried.

I shall never, as long as I live, forget me mam's suffering in those few days. She was wounded to her very bones. They had taken her back to the hospital to identify Little Jess, but once she saw him she had taken him in her arms and would not give him up. She was taking her baby back home.

The nurses and police all tried to separate them, but she would have none of it. Dad never could say how they took him from her, but I reckon that's when she fainted. It had broken me dad's heart to see.

Jessie had been such a mummy's boy. He would always be at her side, pick her the first wild flowers of the year or cuddle up in her arms. We had never done that as kids. Me mam lived till she was eighty-four and never once did she say his name again. Never till the day she died did she get over losing him, nor forgive me dad for his death. On her death bed, her little boy was on her lips.

She never spoke to Pepper again until he was dying, years later. I took her to see him and as we went into his trailer she went to pass him by, but he caught her hand and said, "I'm sorry, Vie."

There were no names, no mention of the accident, but there was no need for them. The three of us all knew what he meant and finally she answered him.

"Alright."

The day after Little Jess' death a man came to the common and asked for 'the Mother'. It was the man who had stopped to pick up me dad and he was quickly taken to me mam, where we all gathered round.

"I want to tell you how your little boy died," he told her, "for I witnessed it from start to finish. I was following this cart, waiting to pass it, but before I could the horse reared up and took off. I saw one man fall off and he quickly got up, running for dear life to catch the horse, shouting and crying. I picked him up to try and get closer, but then we saw a child fall. The back wheel went over him..."

The man explained how they had stopped by the child and jumped from the car. He told me mam what Little Jess had said. Little Jess had died in me dad's arms.

"The boy's father did everything in his power to catch the cart and save his son, but the horse had seemingly gone mad." The man paused, obviously shaken. "I just wanted to tell you," he said and hugged me mam tight before he left.

After the tale had been told, me mam was taken to her wagon. The women whispered amongst themselves, concerned and lost as we were. They said someone was "expecting to go to bed" and "four months" and I soon realised it was me mam the women were whispering about.

So it seemed that she was going to have another child. I was filled with dread.

"Dear Gawd," said one woman. "Look at the state she's in! She'll never do it!"

On and on they went, trying to be kind, but to me it was frightening to hear them talk so. I knew what had happened to Emily and now we had lost Little Jess and soon me mam as well?

The days leading up to the funeral ran into each other until, one afternoon, the Travellers told me mam that a lady was looking for her. When me mam looked up she saw it was her sister Jeannie, who lived in Cheltenham, and she broke down and cried. We had not met any of me mam's family and thought she looked like a lady. Mam's sister Ellen and brother Bobby soon found us too and they never left our sides until we had buried our brother. It was a time we spoke of often, growing up, for we were so close a family that Jessie was missed madly. He would play the big boy during the day, but cuddle up with me like a two-year-old at night.

One day during that long week the chestnut mare was brought onto the common. Bobby took offense that the horse was placed in me mam's sight. "If you don't shoot that horse then I'll do it meself!" he told one and all.

In a flash the horse was gone. I suppose it must have been put down, for it had taken a life and we couldn't keep it with us after that.

There was much coming and going between the common and the villages. Trolley-loads of wood were fetched for the fire and we must have emptied the local shops of tea, sugar and milk. We never ate during our sitting-up time, but gallons of tea were made and passed round by a team of young gals.

It was decided that only me and our Alfie would follow Little Jess, so we were taken off the common and bought new clothes by some relative. Me mam and dad never left the common except to pick out the ground for his grave in the cemetery in Box. We did not have the money to bury our Jess, so me dad's brother Jessie lent me mam the fifty pounds. There would have been a collection round the fire, but me mam was defiant. This was her baby and she would bury him herself. It took her two years to pay Jesse back his money.

Little Jess had had a habit of hiding any coins he was given in a grassy bank or wall for safe-keeping and Alfie, Robert and I knew he had money hidden in the wall at the side of the common. We wanted

Robert gives his brother a farewell kiss.

to place it in with our lost, beloved dead, as a little memento of our lives together. We spent many hours on this secret mission, trying to find his money so that we could give it back to him, but we never found a penny that he'd hidden away. I have always wondered if it was ever found. No one would ever dream that it belonged to a little seven-year-old Traveller boy, who died afore he could spend it.

They brought Little Jess back to the wagons the day afore his funeral. They laid him up in the wagon with the lid off and lit candles for him. It was such a small white box, for he was only little and I remember thinking that little white box was his wagon – his home forever – but oh, he would be lonely without his mam.

It was a long time afore we three got to climb up in our wagon to see our brother, for once me mam had been taken up they couldn't get her out till she passed out in her pain. Then me dad was taken up and he

The final walk. The mourners walking behind Jess's hearse at the start of the two-mile walk to the church. Most of these people had sat up with us for many nights.

too had to be carried back down again. Other grown-ups went up and down until me and our Alfie became worked up, shouting that he was our brother. One at a time we were finally taken up to kiss his dear face.

He looked as though he was sleeping and I wondered why all me mam's sobbing hadn't woken him. I so wanted it to happen – he had been away from us long enough.

All night people went in and out of the wagon, seeing to the candles and checking on Little Jess. Me and our Alfie went up many times. They tried to keep us away, but we were drawn up into the wagon with him. We talked to him and sang his favourite songs. We touched him gently and played with his lovely dark hair, but still he slept on. We tried to shock him by telling him we were searching the wall for his pennies and that we would spend them on sherbet if we found them. It didn't work. Our lovely, cuddly brother was no more – he was too far away to hear us.

We were asked many times what we were up to, to come back down to the fire, but all we wanted was each other. Robert and Emily had long

The last farewell to our little brother Jess. Alfie and I laid our bunches of lily of the valley on his small white coffin.

since fallen asleep and we couldn't get near me mam and dad for all the others looking after them. It was just me and Alfie on that long night. We were strong-willed, the Travellers told each other, let us have our way. One man said about us, "The poor little buggers must feel left out," and that was true enough. We were not young enough to be put to bed, nor old enough to be treated like adults. We floated in the middle and I think that is why that night of awful loss was branded in our memory.

The long night ended and the new day dawned. More tea was handed out and people began to get washed and changed into their black funeral garb. There seemed to be hundreds of people gathered on the common, just waiting in groups. Lorries and pickups arrived, full to the brim with people who wanted to show their respects. Mr Smith and many other non-Travellers were there as well, for all felt our tragedy keenly.

Little Jess was carried out of the wagon for the last time and laid on trestles for us to say our goodbyes. I remember me dad lifting us one after the other to kiss our brother goodbye. It was hard not to go mad.

Alfie and I were dressed and given a bunch of Lily of the Valley each to follow the funeral car. I remember Robert asking to come with us, but he wasn't allowed. We were all warned to behave, but there was no need to warn us. We had become old in the past few days.

It is said to be bad luck to look back in the car, but I just had to as we went slowly down the hill. I was amazed to see such a long line of Travellers, dressed in the deepest black, two abreast. Their heads were down and some carried little children, clutching them tightly. It was a long, two-mile walk down the hill to the cemetery and hard slog back up, but young and old would do it with pride and respect.

The people from the villages lined the way once we reached Box. Newspaper men were snapping photos of our procession – our Little Jess had to die to get so much respect from those villagers.

Chapter Nineteen

On to Devonshire

I T WAS VERY QUIET AND LONELY on the common once all was over. The other Travellers had left apart from Jim and May, Pepper and Amy, but me mam couldn't bear to leave the cemetery. She was out of her mind with grief and we couldn't get her back.

No one was earning any money and I picked up from their talks that things were getting desperate, but I knew that once we left this haunted place we would never return to stop here again.

One morning, me dad announced that he was taking me mam back down to Devonshire, to her family, and she reluctantly agreed. She had lost a lot of weight and looked bad. Me dad offered to chop our wagon away but she would not hear of it and for that me and Alfie were glad. We missed Jess with all of our beings, but when we fell asleep in that wagon we could feel him with us and it was a secret happiness that we never shared with our parents.

We hitched up and pulled out, but as we passed the cemetery me mam leapt from the wagon and ran to Jessie's grave. It took the three men to put her back in the wagon – she was now demented and we were all upset and crying.

We passed the Prince Lane to say farewell to me dear old granddad who gave me mam five shillings towards the grave and a three-legged stool to sit on. We went through Radstock Wells, Glastonbury and the Swine's Jump Road, but never asked about the murderer mush. We stopped on the way through Wellington to sell a few pegs, before finally pulling in on Maiden Down Common near Cullompton.

We stayed there for weeks, me mam finally venturing out calling with her pegs. This common was very different to the one we had left, for it was covered with bracken and purple heather, with lots of young trees. It was on this common that May bored me ears with a needle and cotton, declaring I was now old enough to wear earrings. I was told to sit and pinch me ears till they were numb.

"Will this hurt me, Aunt May?" I asked.

"Not much, but you're a big gal now, Maggie, and it's time you had gold in they ears of yours."

"You ain't gonna hurt me is you, Aunt May?"

"Shut up and come here," she said.

She had boiled the cotton and needle first and then held a cork to the back of me earlobe. She passed the needle through my ear and the cork, threading the string through to make a little cotton earring which I had to pull through the hole several times a day to stop it sticking and growing over.

When both ears were bored she put some Dettol on them and I was told to keep the cotton earrings in until I was given some gold rings to swap them for.

Pepper and Amy soon left the common to turn back, deciding not to come to Devonshire with us. Me mam still couldn't bring herself to look at Pepper, so it was easier for us all once he had left.

One day, when the grown-ups were out calling, a very pretty bow-topped wagon pulled up by us. It belonged to a young couple who spoke funny, or at least we thought so. They had no children with them, so we waited until they had unhitched before we went over to welcome them onto the common. They were very nice to us, asking where our parents were. We told them and watched from a distance as they got on with unpacking, knowing better than to make nuisances of ourselves.

When our lot came home they asked how long the new Travellers had been on the common.

"Not too long, Dad," I answered, "but they talks sort of funny."

"You is daft, my Maggie," he said laughing, but as it turned out they were a young Irish family. When they came over to our fire to greet the others we young ones were fascinated by their lovely sing-song accent.

We stayed with them a couple of weeks until we were getting ready to shift. As we were packing up the young Irish woman asked me mam if I could travel with them awhile. They would meet up later to hand me back, they promised. Well, that did not go down well! Me mam and dad both got fightable, telling the young couple in no uncertain terms how they could get their own children. It was just too close to losing our Little Jess to even think about letting another of us out of their sight.

We went down through Cullompton and Jim and May turned back, saying Devonshire was not for them. It was sad to see them turn their wagons back the next morning and me and our Alfie would miss Jimmy and Lilea.

"Well, my Vie, we's on our own now," me dad said sadly.

"It makes no mind to me, Len," mum answered.

"Well, let's get on the road then," he said, "Gee up, Patchie, let's be having you."

So on we went, further into Devonshire. To me, Alfie and Robert this was new country – it looked and smelt so different to the areas we were used to. Each day was an adventure to us. The roads and lanes were very narrow with heather growing here and there alongside the

Mam's sister Ellen out calling the hotels in Torquay in the Seventies.

bracken. We had found lots of little effets[26] on the common and now caught sight of more of them laying in the sun. How Jimmy had hated those effets – when we had left to fetch water from the middle of the common he would hop, skip and cry at the sight of them. Jimmy had a

26. lizards

bad stutter and we could barely understand him in his fright.

We finally pulled into a lovely little green lane, staying by the wagons while me mam and dad went calling. We spent a few hours nutting – picking the hazel nuts and cracking them with stones by the wagon. We talked about Little Jess often when alone like this, remembering how when nutting he would always fill one pocket for himself and another for his mam.

Me dad would always stop in a place that was well hidden, so that we would be safe left with the wagons while our parents went calling or hawking. The next time we shifted, one of the Newton Abbot Travellers came across us and a message was sent on to Aunt Ellen to let her know we were on our way.

Bob came out in his small lorry to meet us. They were more up-to-date than the 'up-country' Travellers like us, with motorised cars to pull their wagons. Aunt Ellen was over the moon to see me mam. They hugged and cried as they greeted one another.

"Oh, my sis," Ellen cried. "It's good to be with you again! Stay down here, sis – don't go back up that old country again!"

"I won't go back to stay, our Ell," me mam replied, "but I gotta go back to Box in and out."

"I'll ask me dad if you can pull up Golvers Hill with us. He won't say no, my sis, he'll be so glad to have you back!"

Granddad Jimmy Small owned land known as Golvers Hill. It had water on it and was within walking distance of Newton Abbot, which would suit us down to the ground. We agreed to travel on to Kennford and meet Bob and Aunt Ellen in a few days time. At Kennford a farmer took pity on us and let us pull up on one of his fields so me parents didn't have to worry about leaving us during the day.

One afternoon when they were home with us me dad came across the field where he'd been with his horses.

"Vie," he said, shaking his head. "I just seen a funny thing."

"Oh and what's that?" she asked.

Granddad Jimmy Small, a little man with a big heart. Married twice, he had at least seventeen children, had they all lived. Taken at his beloved Golvers Hill.

"You won't believe me. I've just seen your dad and Annie drive past us. They never looked right nor left!" (Annie was me granddad's second wife.)

"No, you're wrong," said me mam. "Me dad wouldn't pass me by."

"Well, if it wasn't they, I must be blind."

We put it down to me dad having been mistaken but later that week Bob and Ellen drove onto the field. Ellen was crying and laughing, so upset that her red hair made her look as if she were on fire.

"That's done it!" she told me mam as she came close. "I told Jimmy Small what he and Annie can do with their field!"

"What's happened, our Ell?" asked me mam.

"They won't have you on their ground," she said.

"But why, my sis? Me dad knows the state I'm in!"

"It's your Lenard. He won't have Lenard on the ground because he'll cut the hedges to pieces cutting peg sticks."

"I shan't go there, then." Me mam nodded to herself. "We can manage."

"I'm pulling out to stop with you," said Ellen. "I told me dad I'm leaving."

"Don't, my sis, you stay with me dad. We'll be alright." Me mam looked at her sister carefully, "but tell me one thing, Ell. Did me dad and Annie pass me by the other day? My Lenard says he's seen 'em."

"Yes, Fiance. They told me they'd seen Lenard in the field with his horses," she confirmed.

Me mam seemed shaken. "My sis," she asked Ell, "would you tell me dad something for me?"

"What is it?"

"Tell me dad," she said fiercely, "that Defiance said 'the ground he got will be there when he's dead and gone'."

"I will," she promised, "and a lot more besides. Now, I want you to shift on to Drum Bridges and pull in. We can both stop there for a bit."

"You shouldn't leave me dad, our Ell," said me mam, though she was grateful.

"I wouldn't stop there now if he paid me!" she answered. "Just you wait till I get back there. I'll make the field ring!"

We didn't doubt her for a second.

Chapter Twenty

A Family Reunion

To get to Drum Bridges from Kennford we had to go through Holden Hill. The hill was long, steep and narrow and it was a real chore to get the wagon up safely.

Ticker was put onto the shafts of the wagon with Patchie as a tracer. I led the young foal, Storm, while our Alfie kept close behind the wagon with the molly block to put behind the wheel if the two horses needed a breather. Me mam walked on ahead with Robert and Emily and we gave them a good head start. We knew once we started the pull up the hill we could wait for no one, as the horses would be working flat out.

It seemed never-ending, but once at the top of the hill we pulled up to let the two horses cool down. They were sweating buckets despite the earliness of the morning.

"Alright, Patchie," soothed me dad. "It's downhill all the way now."

We knew that downhill could be as rough on the horses as up, for they would have the whole weight of the wagon to hold back, but luckily we had a brake on the back wheels and Ticker would still be by Patchie's side to help.

When we finally reached the land at Drum Bridges we found it a pretty place, with young withies growing and a little stream running through. Aunt Ellen and Bob were as good as their word and pulled in right behind us with their lorry and trailer.

Within days me dad had bought a four-square tent, complete with floor-boards and a bed for the two boys, for we were too old now to sleep in the same wagon. A Queenie stove was put into the tent and we were finished. Now only me and Emily would be sleeping under the bed in the wagon.

Me mam gave birth to our Holly on the third of November. They named her for the Christmas wreaths they had been making when me mam went into labour. It was our very first Christmas in Devon.

After Christmas, Robert and me were put into Drum Bridges school, once more relegated into the corner of the classroom. It was not such a bad school. No one was really spiteful to us for the months we were there. It was during this time that our Alfie had his first brush with his powers of foresight. One night, he woke up to see a man standing over him, dressed in a black suit and holding out a tray covered in glasses of wine or some other drink. Alfie was not afraid when he told us of this, though I thought I would've been frit to death. He swore it was more than a mere dream or apparition: someone was in the tent but it wasn't anyone from the family. This would happen again and again throughout his life. When me dad's sister Touwie died, for instance, our Alfie was down in Cornwall racing his bikes, so we couldn't tell him she had died as he was out of contact. But he phoned me to tell me she had died. How did he know? Her spirit rode all the way back up to Somerset with him: he could smell her fag smoke all the way and he just knew it was her. And of course we were able to confirm that he was right.

From Drum Bridges, we shifted on to a part of Dartmoor called Ramshorn Down. This part of the moor has had Travellers stopping on it for many generations. The spot was covered in heather, with a bunch or two of wild snowdrops and daffies peeping out from the thick purple where Travellers before us had dropped or planted the bulbs while sorting their flowers.

We had pulled in to a small quarry tucked away from all winds and weathers and protected by big stones. We were to spend nearly two years on the moor. Alfie was now working with me dad and Bob, but me and Robert were put into a new school, in Bickington.

We were amazed by this new school, for on our first day we were given books, pencils, daps and a dapbag, even a hook to hang up our jackets. The whole school gave us a warm welcome and we never once got segregated from the rest of the children. We couldn't believe our luck as we sat down at our desks with the others. For once we wanted to go to school and me mam never once had to drag us, crying and carrying on.

Me dad had chopped our wagon for a Radar Unit that had been used in the war. It was like a trailer without many windows. It had no kind of heating, so we put a little Queenie inside of it and a bed with a mattress for me and Emily beneath it. It was like having our own trailer of sorts and though we kept the horses for breeding we now had a lorry to tow the trailer with.

Soon me mam announced that she had saved enough to pay Uncle Jessie back for our Little Jess's funeral and so one morning in May me dad kicked off for Wiltshire with the money. He met up with Jessie at the Devizes Fair, paid him his money and got so drunk that he barely made it home to Devonshire. When he finally did return we discovered that he had smashed the lorry into a tree, nevermore to be driven, and walked the rest of the way back to the moor. We were now one lorry short and me mam let him have it – they had to start all over again to save up for another.

One fine day me mam's brother Bobby came to us, full of lush and excited. "Get dressed," he called, "I got someone who wants to meet you!"

He wouldn't take no for an answer, so we all piled into Bobby's lorry. He took us up onto the common at Holden Hill where we saw a fine sight. There were big tents and lorries, and people dressed up in fine clothes all running to meet and greet us.

"This is they," said Bobby, "me two sisters, our Vie and our Ellen." Me mam and Aunt Ell soon disappeared amongst hugs and kisses from the strangers.

A while later we discovered that these Travellers were me mam's long lost aunts and uncles – her real mam Minnie Black's sisters. They had travelled all the way down from Hampshire, looking for Minnie's children. It was an enormous shock and there was great joy for us all on that common. If a stranger had come upon us they would've thought we'd been touched by the moon, so pleased was everyone to meet up with one another at last.

It was a grand week we all had. To us, they seemed very rich people. They had far more than we ever had but were kind and lovely people. I have forgotten many of their names but never the Travellers themselves.

After so much sadness, it was a wonderful time for us. Me mother told them all of Little Jess and the grief we were suffering and though she didn't sing with them, she drank and chattered to the early hours.

Before they left, the women took me mam and Aunt Ellen out and bought them a lovely piece of china each. They treasured these keepsakes, for soon these new members of our family were gone and we were left to get on with our lives again. After all the parties on the common, it seemed a bit lonely, but we made the best of our road.

We were enjoying living on the moor, where the world was wild and wonderful, full of endless colour and wildlife, but all the bustle of meeting new people had given me dad itchy feet. He wanted to shift back up country where his own family were, for me mam's family had never taken well to him.

Me and our Robert would miss that little school in Bickington that had welcomed us so fully and all the old tales that Aunt Ellen told us round the fire at night.

My favourite story was of a gal called Kitty Jay. She had been taken out of the workhouse to be a skivvy on a local farm many years ago. The farmer's son soon fell for her and decided to take her as a lover. Soon she was 'expected to go to bed' – she was going to have a baby. The villagers turned against her and the farmer's son blamed her for their situation and, not knowing what else to do, Jay hanged herself.

Jay had been buried by a crossroads out on the moor and Ellen had taken us to put wild flowers on her grave, as she had often done as a child. Many Travellers have kept this tradition for decades, going to the secluded little spot to place fresh flowers on her lonely grave. More recently the grave has been built up and many visitors to the moor stop and leave flowers at the girl's resting place.

Another strange tale that Ellen told was of an old gal and her man who lived years ago in a rod tent. Late one evening, the man of the family was putting up his rod tent in a farmer's gateway in the outskirts of Newton Abbot. He went to fetch wood and water, leaving his family safe and sound with the tent.

While he was gone, the mam fed her two small children and put them to bed in the tent. She sat round the fire, waiting for her man to come back. Suddenly, she heard a grunting noise. She looked up and down the dark lane, but could see nothing suspicious.

Still, it worried her and she built up the fire to make flames, in case it was some nasty mumper looking to make trouble.

Soon she heard the noise again and once more left the fire to look up and down the lane. There in front of her, trotting up the lane, she saw a spotted pig! That made her laugh. Fancy letting a pig put the wind up her. The pig stopped and tried to turn into the gateway where her tent was blocking him off. The mam shooed the pig away, trying to keep it out of the tent in case it scared her children.

The pig was determined to get through that gate, so she picked up a stick off the fire that was well alight and hit the pig to shoo it away. She realised that the more she beat the pig, the bigger it got.

Soon the pig got past her and ran right through the tent, ripping the back out. She was relieved to find that her children had slept right through it, unhurt, and soon her man came back and she told him all that had happened.

The next morning the farmer came up the lane and the young mam stopped him to explain. "I'm very sorry sir, but I had to beat one of your pigs last night. I'm sorry to say he must be black and blue, for he runned right through me tent!"

The farmer looked hard at her and said, "Miss, you never beat my pig. That was the Devil."

"The Devil?" cried the Traveller woman.

"That pig's been seen and beat afore in this lane and no one is safe who stops here – you're very lucky to still be in one piece!"

Dartmoor had a hundred of these old tales, or so it seemed, and how we would miss them if we had to move on now!

Me mam tried to talk me dad out of shifting. "Let me baby get a bit older?"

Baby Holly was only a few months old, already a dark-haired beauty and good as gold. After school I would put her on me hip and take her for walks, showing her the mice in the quarry. (Our Alfie had let a load of white mice loose in the quarry and they had bred with the wild ones – they were everywhere.)

"I've been in this country long enough," said me dad, "so make your mind up. We's shifting back next week."

He was resolute. We would soon be moving on.

Chapter Twenty-one

Village Life

ME DAD WON THE ARGUMENT and we soon began to shift ourselves from that beloved place. First, our three horses were taken back up to a field me dad had used before. They had never been in a lorry before and were hard to load up for they were so upset. We knew that, with the horses gone, our time would be short on the moor.

Aunt Ellen was so upset that we were shifting back. She and me mam promised to find someone who could write letters for them and stay in touch that way. We visited the Smalls to say our farewells and left Ellen in floods of tears.

With the lorry we returned to Wiltshire much faster than it had taken us to travel down – hours instead of weeks. Baby Holly and Emily rode in the front of the lorry with mam and dad, while we three were packed in the back.

"I don't want to go," said Alfie. "Do you?"

"No, our Alfie. I never wanted to leave that school," I told him. I was starting to do really well, I had thought. We had made friends there and got on well with the teachers.

"Neither did I," Robert piped up. "It was the bestest school we been to and they said they wished we could stay – remember?"

"We shan't never find another school like that one," I said unhappily.

We never did find another like it. The next school I went to was Pensford, not far from Chelwood Bridge. We pulled into a lane nearby and stayed there some weeks until me mam and dad got to know a lady who owned a paddock in a little village called Compton Dando. She agreed for us to stay as long as we liked, so we were off again.

We were put to school down in the village. It took some weeks before the children would play with us, but it came right in the end. Just as I was getting used to the place I was sent on to the big school in Keynsham. I had to be picked up by taxi and I hated that nearly as much as the school. The school was huge and seemed to have hundreds of classrooms. I found I was out of me depth, floundering like fish out of water and nobody wanted to know me there. I was lonely on me own, without our Robert.

I was sat in class one day, looking out the window at a gang of girls playing ball with sticks, when I was brought up short by the teacher man shouting at me.

"You're no use in here! If you want to be out there then get out of my classroom!"

That was all I needed to hear, so I got up and walked out to much laughter from the other children. I walked round to the field and approached this woman with a whistle in her mouth.

"The man said I can play ball with you," I told her.

"Did he now?" she asked me. "Well, can you play hockey?"

"Yes, I can play it," I said. It looked easy enough – all you needed to do was hit the ball about. I was given a stick and went mental with it, beating the ball up and down until I found that I was being beat as much as the ball was! I didn't understand what was up with all that lot – I was scoring goals, wasn't I? And here's these gals trying to break me dear, skinny legs!

"What's up with you?" I hollered at a girl who delivered a mighty blow to me with her stick. "I'll hit you back, you spiteful cow!"

The woman teacher collared me, going on about teams.

"I'm doing a good job, ain't I?" I asked her.

"But you're playing for both teams. You can only play for one!"

"What's a team, then?" I asked and was sent off the field. Instead of going back into that old school I walked the seven or eight miles home, only to get in trouble with me mam for walking out.

"They ain't nice to me, mam," I cried, trying to make her understand. "I don't like being in that school on me own!"

"If you don't go, my Maggie, the school mush will take you off and put you in a bad gals' home."

"You wouldn't let him!"

"I'd have no say in it!" she said. "Come Monday I'll come in with you and see what's going on in there, now be a good gal."

"You won't!" I hollered. "I know you won't – you're just saying it!"

"Strike me dead, I'll come."

The next Monday I was sent for by the head mush. True to her word, me mam was sat in that little office and I was pleased to see her, sure she'd take me home. No such luck, though. I was here to stay.

The head mush told her I was useless. Here I was, twelve years old and could hardly write me own name, let alone do anything else. He told me mam I shouldn't be in his school and I agreed. I should've been home, cooking and cleaning and going out calling, but the law said I had to be in that school. He said it wasn't fair on the other students, as I disrupted the classes I was in.

He spoke of me like I was a fool or worse and school never got any better for me. I thought it was a waste of life to be trapped inside that big building.

Outside of school, life in the village was wonderful. We had got to know two boys called John and Richard Hodinot and a young lad called Michael Barns, who rode a bike from Bristol every Friday night to stay the weekend with his auntie, Annie Hatcher, who lived nearby us.

We had such fun with these three boys that we were hardly ever home in the new trailer me dad had chopped the Radar Unit for.

We taught the boys how to catch the stickleback fish that hid under the big stones in the river and how to climb trees to see the baby pigeons and owls in their nests and – funniest of all – we taught them how to ride a horse bareback. Me dad had the most cantankerous pony that ever lived. He acted mild and sweet-natured and would let you climb on his back and then he'd take off for the nearest hedge and buck you right in, over his head. We had many hours of fun with him and the boys especially loved him despite the scratches that covered their arms and legs.

On a Saturday night me mam and dad would book up the taxi and take us all to Keynsham to see the pictures. When the Queen's Coronation rolled around, the village invited our family to watch it on the little television in the village hall. We had never seen a box that showed pictures before and enjoyed every minute of it. We were even given a mug with the young couple's faces painted on it. Oh it was a lovely day and the village was decorated with flags and bunting.

Life went on this way for some time, until one day me dad came home all excited. He had bought a piece of land.

"Oh, we ain't got to shift again?" we groaned.

"Yes we is," he said, "and this time it will be our own ground and no police or anyone else can move us on."

"Where's it at?" we asked. Me mam and dad just looked at each other. We asked again, "Where's it at?"

"Climb up the back of the lorry and we'll show you," said me dad.

We took this for bad news and sullenly helped our parents shift us on. We would be leaving the only non-Romani friends we had ever had, but go we must.

We drove through the familiar lanes until our Alfie turned to me with a frown.

"Hang on a minute," Alfie said, realising we were close to the Prince Lane. "We's heading for Peasedown St John. See, this is Camerton!"

"Oh Lord, Alfie – he wouldn't, would he?"

Sure enough, we headed down a lane called Keel's Hill in the village of Peasedown St John, only to stop halfway down.

"Where's the ground then?" we asked, for all we could see were high hedges and brambles. Me dad pointed out an overgrown strip of land, long and narrow. It ran nearly the full length of the hill.

"You can't get our trailer in there, dad," I told him. "We'll be stifled with the brambles and Prince Lane is just down the road."

"Hark your gab, Maggie. You always got too much to say for yourself."

"But dad, we can't stick this old village, can we, Alfie? And the granny's just down the road!"

"I'm telling you, Maggie – I bought this bit of ground for you lot!"

"Well, you could've bought it somewheres else," I answered back.

"Now look here, little woman," me mam told me. "I hope you got as much to say when I put you in the village school!"

From there we drove down the lane to visit me old granddad. We hadn't seen him for some time and he looked old and withered, though he was happy to see us. At least with the new land we would be in walking distance and could see the poor old man more often.

There were lots of the family to greet us as we pulled up in the lane. Tom and Kizzie, Alfie and Dillion, John and Ellen and Joe and Ally were all gathered around one big fire and there sat me granny with her old pipe hanging from the corner of her mouth. She was poking a long, two-pronged fork at a bit of bacon in the frying pan and the smell made my stomach growl with hunger. She sat at the fire with smoke blowing in her face. I could feel her eyes on us and was waiting to hear the old call to fetch her wood and water.

Me dad told the family about Keel's Hill and they were pleased as punch for him. Me old granny's face lit up as well and I wondered what she'd have in store for us.

"Well, our Lenard," Joe told him, "you're a landowner at last."

John promised to help us clear the bushes and brambles that covered our new land and help us move on, and, sure enough, only a few weeks later we were ready to shift onto the bit of ground.

Me dad had bought us a big hut that used to be a village shop and rebuilt it on the ground. We had water and electric put in and, for the first time since that squatters' hut, a permanent address.

It was 22 Keel's Hill, Peasedown St John, Nr Bath.

Soon, me and our Robert were sent to Peasedown School. This village knew 'Gypsies' well and so straightaway the other children decided I would pay for being one. That first week I suffered dearly – I was punched, spat on, kicked. It all seemed to stem from one boy and I knew that I had to conquer that villain myself or live in misery, for there was no use in me running home crying.

I decided to try and finish it on a Friday. I walked out of class just before home time and waited with me heart in me mouth for the boy to leave the school. Alfie had always taught me that you stood a good chance so long as you got the first punch in, so as the boy came out of the gate laughing with his mate, I punched him between his two eyes.

He was not expecting that and suddenly – Gawd alone knows how – I had him down and was laying into him. Like most bully boys, he couldn't take his own medicine and ran off. I never squeaked a word of what I'd done to that boy when I got home, knowing that come Monday I would either be free or trapped even worse. At least I wasn't afraid of him any more.

That evening, we had just finished our bit of supper when a man started shouting for me dad to come out. He was black with coal dust and his eyes blazed angrily.

"Bloody Gypsies beating up on my son!" he hollered. "Come out, you bloody Gyppo!"

We all rushed outside and me heart fell to me belly. Standing behind that big mush was the bully boy.

"What's up, panch-mouth?" asked me dad. "Who's you hollering at?"

"You!" shouted the man. "Just look at how your Gypsy bastards have served my son!"

Me dad took a good long look at we three and I couldn't hide the guilt from my face. "Come here, Maggie," he said quietly and I obeyed. "Did you do that?"

I said nothing, but the man started shouting again. "No she did not, it was all your lot!"

"I'll asks you once more, Maggie. Did you do this?"

Me dad knew it had to be me. Alfie and Robert would've probably bragged had they done it, but no matter. However he knew, I had to tell the truth.

"Yes," I admitted, "but he asked for it! He's been punching and beating me ever since I set foot in that school!"

"Well, mister, what have you to answer to that?" asked me dad, his eyes alight.

"She never done it," hollered the mush. "Not on her own she didn't!"

"I did do it!" I cried. "He's a real villain, dad!"

The man grabbed hold of his son and dragged him forward. "Tell this man which of them done this to you and I'll see if the father can treat me the same. I won't bloody well stand for your guttersnipes to beat my son!"

There was nothing for it. I stepped up to the boy full of fury. "You know full well I blacked your eyes for what you've been doing to me all week."

"Is that true?" asked his dad.

"Yes," said the boy, "but wait till Monday! I'll kill you in school, you dirty Gyppo!"

"Well," said me dad, smiling now. "You got a boy there to be proud of. He let a little skin an' bone gal give him a hiding." Me dad squared up to the mush. "Want me to give you the same treatment?"

The man could not believe his son's confession and completely ignored me dad in favour of beating his boy all the way back down the hill. "Fighting with a girl!" we heard him shout. "Letting her get the best of you!"

Our lot fell about laughing at the sound of it, till me mam turned a stern glare on me. "Maggie, I wants a word with you."

I knew me dad would not let her hit me, for I'd only done what they'd been telling me to do all these years. I had finally stood up for myself without relying on any other. I thought I now knew a little of how our Alfie had felt, that first day at the squatters' hut, when he had taken on his nightmare and won.

Chapter Twenty-two

Planning Permission

S CHOOL WAS NOT SO BAD after that. The boy gave me a wide
berth and so most of the other bullies did too. Over the coming
years, his dad and mine actually became firm friends. They
often went flapping with their greyhounds together.

We still left the ground to go pea- and hop-picking, or to the horse fairs,
taking the trailer to sleep in. Me dad was proud that his little chicks were
all growing up – we could now work a full day in the pea fields and hop
gardens and it made a real difference to our pay. Me dad worked with Dan
and Jim dropping rag-bills and once he got on his feet a bit he bought an
old Dormobile van. He'd take us all out to the beach at Weymouth, or to
Cheddar to climb the rocks. It was these trips that we relied on to keep us
sane, for none but me mam could stay in one place for too long. Our feet
would itch as we waited for the seasons to come round.

Though the police could no longer shift us from the land we owned,
we hadn't reckoned with the council. One morning, a man came to the
ground and told me dad that we couldn't stop there unless we had
planning permission.

"What's you on about?" asked me dad. "I owns this ground – I bought and paid for it!"

"You still cannot live on it," said the man. Me mam's face turned white as a sheet and me dad was growing agitated.

"Let's hear what he's got to say," me mam said.

Me dad shook his head. "I can hear what he's saying: we've gotta shift. Well, I owns this ground and I ain't shifting for nobody!"

"Oh dear, he'll hit that mush in a minute," our Alfie whispered to me.

Keeping a close eye on me dad, the man explained to me mam that in order to live on the land we needed to put in a planning application.

"What's that then?" she asked him.

"It's a form you have to fill in and take to the council office."

"Then if I does that I can bide here?"

"I don't know – but the council will decide once they have all the facts."

"What bloody facts?" asked me dad. "The fact is this: I'm stopping here."

"Hark, my Len," me mam snapped, "the mush will get you locked up."

"Well let him – I ain't done nothing wrong."

"You moved onto this land without planning permission," the man said again. Me dad swore and hollered at him as walked away to his car and drove off.

Me mam was crying big tears as she turned away. "You done well there, Lenard!"

"What's you on about?" me dad cried. "Is you deaf and dumb? Who does he think he is? I own this ground!"

They fought long and hard over the man's visit, until me dad got in the lorry and drove off in a temper. Once he left, me mam started pacing like a mad thing. She had made this nice place that she was proud of – her own home – and now she was about to lose it.

Eventually, she called me to her. "Maggie, I wants you to do something for me. You know that lady that always stops to speak – the one with two boys?"

"Mrs Frogley, you mean? Her that lives down in Carlingcott?"

"That's her. Run down and find out if she will come up and see me."

Carlingcott was over a mile away but, seeing the state me mam was in, I ran like a March hare. When I finally got to the woman's house and found her at home I breathed a sigh of relief, for I knew that, had she not been home, me mam would've had me running back and forth like a yo-yo all day!

"Please lady, me mam said could you come up, urgent like?"

She looked at me in alarm. "Whatever is wrong? Is your mother ill?"

"She will be if you don't come soon!" I told her.

Poor Mrs Frogley walked all the way back with me and once there me mam took the kind woman with her into the hut to tell her the gist of what the council man had said.

"Oh I know what he wants," said Mrs Frogley. "You have to get planning permission to live here – I know what to do!"

"Do you?" cried me mam. "Will you help me, then?"

"Yes of course! First we must get the planning forms and then I'll help you fill them in. Then we'll take them ourselves or post them to the council offices."

"Where do I get the forms?" asked me mam.

"The council offices in Bath," Mrs Frogley replied. "Get yourself ready and we'll take the bus now."

"Oh, you is a kind woman," me mam told her as she rushed to gather her things.

Later that day the two women were like lawyers, meticulously filling out those forms before getting them off to the post office. Me mam thought that was the end of it and we would now be stopping there for good.

"That's a load off me mind!" she said, when all was posted, "and you lot ain't no more use than ornaments. All that schooling you've had and you can't write your own names!" Me dad finally returned and mam told him, "It's alright, Len. I sorted it."

"That's alright, then," he replied. "If that council man comes back aggravating me, he'll come to no good!"

Weeks passed and we thought no more of it, but one day the man returned. The hut had not been passed by the council. It would have to go.

"What is you on about now?" hollered me dad. "I gotta take me hut down?"

"I'm afraid so," the man explained. "It's not made on wheels and so must be taken down."

Me dad was bewildered. "Is you taking the mick out of me? Have you ever seen a wooden shop hut on wheels?"

"No I haven't," he answered, "but I'm telling you, it has to go."

"And I'm telling you that you're off your head!" said me dad. "So if this hut had wheels you would let it bide here?"

"Yes," said the man.

"Well, mister," me dad answered. "You come back next week and it'll have wheels on it."

Over the next few days me dad went out and got himself dozens of little wheels – the kind normally used on chicken coops – and nailed them onto the bottom of the hut, painting them black so that they could be seen. By the time he'd finished with it that hut looked like a train on the tracks. Love him, he was proud of what he'd done, though like the rest of us he did not realise that the man had meant the hut should have a chassis under it. When the council man returned he could not believe his eyes! He kept walking around the hut, shaking his head and muttering to himself.

"You wanted wheels, you got wheels!" me dad told him.

"I most certainly have," he replied with a bewildered look. The poor man didn't know quite what to make of it. "Tell me, could you tow this thing? With these wheels on?"

"Mister," said me dad, "I could tow this hut a hundred mile."

Sure enough, the man wrote that in his little book, bid us good day and left. Weeks later a letter arrived, granting us planning permission! Finally, thanks to Mrs Frogley and me dad's wheels, it was all sorted – no more sleepless nights for me mam.

That planning application must have gone down in Bath's history – it certainly stayed in my mind, and me dad was like a peacock for months. It was the first time that he had gone up against the council and won anything. As time went on those little iron wheels slowly fell off the hut and were weighed in with the scrap until there were none left, but still we remained on our own bit of land.

Chapter Twenty-three

Growing Up

THE YEARS PASSED BY QUICKLY on that little bit of land. I had learned a grand sod all at the local school and was transferred to Writhlington New School, near Radstock. At fifteen I left to get a job doing the milk round. Our Alfie got a job down the coalmine at Writhlington and soon bought his first motorbike. Me mam had two more children at Keel's Hill, Maralyn and Richard, which brought us to seven. If we had not lost Little Jess we would have been eight.

Poor Uncle Tom died in 1955 and was buried at Paulton. His tent was burned with all his belongings, leaving Kizzie and the children with hardly a thing to their names. We lost our poor lovely granddad soon after. As they took him off to hospital for the last time he turned his head to us and said, "Goodbye, Prince Lane," which made every one of us cry. Granddad passed away in St Martin's Hospital, Bath and was laid to rest in Paulton cemetery with the rest of the family. The old granny stayed on down the lane, but all the family took turns to stop with her and care for her.

That little mush our Alfie who lived for motorbikes. Taken at Keel's Hill.

Granddad left a big gap in all our lives. No more would we hear his old tales from years gone by, though we shared as many as we could in the days after, and I have passed a few on myself over the years.

Once, in their younger days, granddad and the old granny were pulled up on a road near Bristol. They had been there a couple of days and each evening he had to outwit the farmer to poove his gry[27]. He would wait until the farmer was a-bed and then walk his horse to the man's seed field. All night long the horse would be able to eat the best grass in the field, until me granddad would collect the horse again before the farmer woke on the morrow. This was an old practice of ours, to borrow a field for the horses. Many farmers would do their utmost to catch us out and punish us.

On this night, granddad had sat round the fire much longer than usual before taking his horse to poove, for the full moon was bright in

---

27. Put his horse out to graze.

the sky and it was light enough for the farmer to catch him easily. It was very late when he finally unchained his horse and began leading it down the road in the moonlight. Suddenly, the horse stopped dead in its tracks.

"What's up with you?" me granddad asked as he tugged at the horse. "Don't you want to fill your belly up?"

Still the horse did not want to move. Granddad pulled hard on the halter to bring the wary horse a few more yards but it resisted, shaking and showing the whites of its eyes.

Granddad was mystified as he tried to work out what was up. He looked up and down the road, trying to find whatever had spooked the horse, when he spotted two little children.

"What the hell is they doing out so late?" he asked the horse. They were easy to see in the moonlight, with coats wrapped round them and school satchels on their backs. They were walking down the road away from him, all on their own. Me granddad shook his head.

"This ain't right," he muttered. "Their mother wants beating, letting two young 'uns wander the roads at night!" He called out to the two children. "Hey, wait up! I'll take you both back home!"

They ignored him and walked on, though me granddad dragged hard at his horse trying to catch them up. Feeling at a loss as to what to do, me old granddad took the horse back to the wagon and put him on the chain. He sat by the fire, puzzling over why two little children would be wandering around so late at night. "Emma," he called to me granny, "you won't believe me, but I just went to poove me gry and there was these two little children walking down the road!"

"What time is it?" she asked.

"Must be gone eleven by now," he said.

"Then get yourself off to bed – you been seeing things."

"No I ain't, I seen them plain as day!"

"You're off your rocker," me granny said. "Get to sleep. You gotta be up soon to fetch the horse."

"No I ain't, he wouldn't be pooved. I had to fetch him back."

Me dad's brother Tom died of TB. Everything he owned was burnt on the evening of his funeral, January 25th 1955 (above and right).

"Then he's as barmy as you is," said me granny and went off back to sleep.

The next morning me granddad still felt uneasy as he packed up to shift. They pulled out, going the way those two children had gone and when they came to a cottage granddad pulled up to speak to a man in his garden.

"Did your two little 'uns get back safe and sound last night?" he asked.

"What little 'uns are they?" questioned the man.

"Those two children that was out half the night! If they was your two, you should be horsewhipped for not looking after 'em!"

The man looked surprised and stopped what he was doing to walk closer to me granddad. "What did they look like?"

Granddad described what he'd seen, telling the man it was shameful

Tent-Home Blazes In Romany Rite

NEARLY 100 gypsies returned to Dunkerton, on Monday afternoon, after a funeral at Paulton, and watched while the dead man's tent was sprinkled with paraffin and set on fire. According to Romany custom, his household possessions were also destroyed in the blaze— within a few minutes only the tent poles, which were burning on the bed, remained.

The funeral was that of Mr. Tom Smith, of Dunkerton Hill, whose body was followed on foot by a long line of his mourning relatives and friends from Paulton Parish Church to the cemetery.

The gypsies went to Paulton from various parts of the district by coach, lorry and car—as well as on foot.

The flowers and wreaths placed on the grave were some of the most beautiful seen in the village for some time. Nearly every floral tribute included spring flowers, with daffodils and tulips in abundance.

A number of these tributes were in the shape of hearts or cushions, and one of the most attractive and unusual was a wreath depicting the open gates of Heaven.

The Rev. L. Jarman (vicar of Ston Easton and Farrington Gurney) officiated at the church and graveside.

that those little children had been out all on their own so late.

"A boy and a girl?" said the man, shaking his head.

"Yes, I seen them clear as day!"

"Well let me tell you," said the man. "You did see two children last night and this is where they lived, years ago! Those two little mites were murdered on their way home from school many years back and it was their spirits that you saw last night. They've been seen from time to time."

This tale amazed me granddad, for he told us that the children were so real to look at. He had even spoke to them – they were real, living beings to his mind that night.

Soon after he started work in the coalmine, our Alfie got himself a girlfriend, which meant I was grounded, for I was only allowed out with him. Me mam and dad were very strict and we gals did not go out unless our brothers were there with us. I was very resentful that this new girl took up so much of his time, whereas before Alfie had often taken me to the pictures and the park.

I didn't like being hemmed in and when the village fair came in for the week, I managed to sneak up there. The village fair was the highlight of the year. It would come for a week, pulling in on the playing fields, and folks would come from all the outlying villages. I wandered around, dressed up in me mam's high-heeled shoes and feeling very grown-up and free – until our Alfie spotted me!

Seeing me chatting to a boy, Alfie gave me a hard clip round the ear. He said me mam had sent him to look for me, telling him to kick me up the arse and send me home. Of course, she had done no such thing, but Alfie insisted. Not liking how my brother had treated me, the boy turned to give him what for.

I left for home as the two boys got fighting, rolling on the ground. When I finally got back I told me mam, who said it was my own fault for going up there without any of me brothers.

"Can I take our Emily up to the fair, then?" I asked plaintively.

"No," she said.

"Can I find our Robert and go up with him, then?"

"No."

"What can I do then, mam?"

"Clean the place up," she said. "Peel the tatters. There's plenty for you to do, my gal!"

The story of me life, I thought. Work, work, work, and not allowed to have any fun at all!

Throughout that summer the Traveller boys started to call on me mam and dad as an excuse to talk to me. Some of them were young, good-looking boys most gals would give their eye teeth for, but when they asked me to go out with them the answer was always no – and not only from me mam! I had my own reasons for not wanting to court a Traveller boy. I had been to the pictures many times with them, but only ever as a big group.

Although they all asked me out, I could see that they were all interested in controlling me. I had picked up a lot of me mam's ways and would get many remarks from the boys telling me that I wouldn't be allowed to wear make-up when I had a man, that me skirt was too short, me hair was styled wrong. Oh, these Traveller boys, for all their good looks, would not be controlling Maggie! I had made me mind up about that!

Me dad put it down to me schooling, but it went far deeper than that. My identity was me own and those Traveller boys would not cow me down, even if I ended up an old maid with no man of me own. Besides, I could never see me dad letting me get married. I was his little gal. I was not alone though – all Traveller parents were strict with their girls and it seemed to me that Traveller men were just as strict with their wives.

I had witnessed the rows between me mam and dad when he tried to change her, I had seen her made an outcast by some of me dad's family – being called a 'painted doll' all for a bit of lipstick and powder. No, I would not be bullied – I was what I was and could not change myself.

That winter, the police came to Keel's Hill with a message for me dad and a phone number to ring. His brother Dan was in trouble and needed help.

Dan had married a woman called Lil from Worcester and they had been travelling up to Kidderminster to stop awhile with Lil's family. One day, Dan's lorry would not start in the bitter cold and so Lil and her mother had started to push the lorry so that Dan could jump-start the engine. His mother-in-law had slipped in the deep snow and fallen under the wheel and died.

It had been an accident, but Lil's family would not hear of it. Dan had killed their mother, as far as they saw it, and now he needed someone to fetch him back to Somerset for his own safety.

Mam and dad left us at home while they went to fetch him. They returned in the early hours of the morning, Dan's wagon roped down on the back of our lorry and all of them crammed in the cab. Dan's lorry must have been burnt down because it had taken a life and although the police had ruled it an accident it was many a year before Dan dared to go back up to that part of the country.

So life carried on. Dan once again worked with me dad, trying to get back on his feet. They earned money trading scrap, dropping rag-bills and pea-picking when the season came round. We would take the trailer and a tent down to Bridgwater to stop with all the other Travellers, Alfie staying behind to look after Keel's Hill. Of course my job went for I would have to go with them. Had I been a boy I could have stayed behind like our Alfie.

Then I got a job at Purnell's of Paulton, a book-printing place. I never took too kindly to being shut in that big place. During me breaks I would take me dinner down to the cemetery and visit me granddad, Emmy and Tom while I ate. It was a funny way to carry on, but I was so close to their graves it made sense to me to visit them.

It was at Purnell's that I met my first boyfriend, John. He was a really nice lad who sent messages to me through one of the other women I worked with. He wasn't a Traveller, but was determined he was going to take me out, however long it took for me to agree – and it took months! I had to lay the groundwork at home and dared not see him alone. Me mam refused to let me see him at all. We had already had one upset with me cousin Emmy, who had asked me aunt Kizzie if she could court a man. It had caused blue murder, for just like John, the boy wasn't one of us.

Emmy had brought him down to meet me mam and dad, hoping to get their support, but Kizzie had come storming down the road, foaming at the mouth, plaits hanging loose and cussing like a man.

"Where is they?" she'd demanded. "I knows they's here!"

Me mam had pushed the lad, Norman, under her bed to keep him from sight. "Who?" she asked, all innocence.

"Our Emmy and that four-eyed mush she got!"

"Emmy's here, but she's on her own." Me mam pointed to the trailer. "Come in and see for yourself."

Kizzie was not satisfied, though, and searched for poor Norman who lay shaking under me mam's bed as Emmy cried. Emmy ended up marrying him in secret, poor gal, and I was terrified that I'd be in for the same thing – all that lying and deceit.

"Why can't we just choose our own men?" I asked, time and again. I begged and pleaded for them to at least meet him and at last I was told to tell John to come and see me dad. I'll never forget that first visit. Talk about being shown up! John pulled up on his motorbike and took off his helmet. He was ginger.

"Ginger!" said me dad. "Just you look and see what my gal been and brought back to me! What have I done to deserve this lot, eh?"

"But it's a nice ginger, dad," I said, not knowing where to put me face. John must've thought we were all bonkers as he looked from one person to the next.

Me dad launched into the interrogation. "How much money have you got? What do you earn? Where do you work? Have you got a police record?" He wasn't happy – his gal had brought home a ginger mush!

He'd rather I kept to our lot, but I wouldn't hear of it.

John promised me dad he would bring no trouble to me and finally me parents gave in, with a few dire warnings of what would happen to John if I brought home any trouble. With a last lecture on how John would never understand my family, our ways or our language, he finally allowed the boy to take me out. I had to be home by eight o'clock, just when everyone else was heading out for the evening, but it was still freedom of a sort.

Having a boyfriend broke a bit of the hold our Alfie had over me. No more paying me brother to take me to the pictures or rides on the back of his motorbike. I still remember the first time I climbed on the bike, early one morning in the fall of the year. It was crispy-cold and frosty as we left for Devonshire to visit Granddad Jim. It was grand to start with, till Alfie pulled up and threatened to beat me if I kept sitting so straight through the corners of the road. How was I supposed to know you were meant to lean in with the bike when it turned?

"You is trying to kill us both dead!" he yelled.

"I ain't, our Alfie – what's you on about?"

"You!" he said. "With they spider's legs! You ain't riding me bike proper."

"Well how's I supposed to ride the bloody bike, then?" I asked.

"Follow me, you great fool. When I bends on a corner, you bend as well."

"The bike'll fall in the road!" I shouted.

"Do you wants to come or do you wants to walk back home?" he asked me. I knew he meant it too. I had to obey him if I wanted to go to Devonshire.

"I wants to come," I said and with a smack round me lugs Alfie let me back on the bike. Miles and miles I hung onto his back, frit to death as we bent into corners, up and down hills.

"Is we lost?" I hollered into his ears, barely hearing his reply.

"No! Shut up and hang on!"

How he ever found his way that day is beyond me, but we finally pulled into Golvers Hill.

"Get off and open the gate," he told me, but when I did manage to inch me way off the seat I was frozen to the shape of the bike.

"I can't move me legs!" I cried.

"Open the gate or you'll walk home!" he hollered back, not realising that granddad Jim was standing over the hedge listening.

"Don't you hurt her, Alfie! I can hear you, boy." Jim opened the gate as we jumped in shock. The bike roared as Alfie spun it through the gate, but I had a job getting me legs to move. I was bitter cold and stiff as anything, so granddad had to help me up to his hut where Annie made us warm tea and a bacon sandwich to warm us up. It was good to see them again.

The need to travel never really left us, no matter how long we stayed at Keel's Hill, and so trips like that were a relief. Sometimes we would stand out on the road, longing to pack up and travel again. One day, as I was heading to the village shop, a couple of old wagons went through the village. How I longed to run behind them, to sit round a wood fire and smell the smoke.

As soon as the pea- and hop-picking seasons came around, our jobs were thrown up and we were off, not returning to Peasedown for weeks or months. Going away was the highlight of each year, but life out on the road was getting more and more difficult as the police stepped up their harassment. Other Travellers told us awful tales about being moved on, hopping from common to common to get a little peace. The police were beginning to move wagons off the grass verges and lanes that we had stopped on for hundreds of years, places we had thought were safe and sacred.

"You don't know how lucky you are, owning your own bit of ground," people told me dad. He heard the same thing again and again. "You can come and go whenever you like."

Still, he would rather have been out travelling. It was hard to earn a living staying in one place. We were restricted in where we could drop the rag-bills and look for scrap – but Keel's Hills was ours and that's where we would stay for many years.

Chapter Twenty-four

A New Life

EVENTUALLY, ALFIE GOT MARRIED and moved into a place in the village. I met a lad called Terry Bendell soon after and we too were married. Me dad went mad. Terry was a gorgie mush from Bristol, so me dad vowed not to come to the wedding and refused to sign the marriage form. Without his signature I couldn't be wed, as I wasn't yet twenty-one, so I signed his name myself.

On the morning of me wedding, much to my delight, every jack man of my family turned up at Bristol registry office. It was a grand day. Me dad gave me new husband a lecture on how to look after me, which came as no surprise to me at all.

We ended up with a flat in the middle of Bristol and I found my new city life very hard. Soon I was expecting to go to bed – having my first child – and was over the moon when I discovered that we weren't allowed to have children in the flat. It was my chance to change things. While my man was at work I rode around on the bus, looking for trailer parks. I found one site that I loved, but we had to buy a trailer to put on it. I was worried about breaking the news to Terry, as we didn't have the money to buy a trailer, but I plucked up the courage to have it out with him.

"It sounds alright," he told me, to my surprise. "I wouldn't mind living on a caravan park, but where's the money going to come from to buy a caravan?"

"Would you trust me to get it?" I asked him.

"I won't borrow off your dad," Terry told me sternly.

"Nor would I – but with your help I can get the money."

He laughed. "How are you going to earn hundreds of pounds?"

"I want you to find out where the rubbish lorries tips the rubbish off to."

"What on earth are you on about?" He asked, still laughing.

"I wants to know where the rubbish tips are round Bristol!" I cried and he dared not go against me. He found out for me and I began collecting some sack bags together for scrap. One evening, he took me to the first tip. He thought I was off me head.

"I'll show you how I can earn me living," I smiled. "Follow me." I taught my man what scrap metal was: brass, copper, aluminium, zinc and gun-metal. We collected it all, placing it in separate bags. We headed to the scrapyard for my first weigh-in of my very own and Terry got a shock when I weighed off my car boot full of metals. So much money for so little; he could not believe his luck.

We continued this most evenings, weighing off on a Saturday morning. We went further and further afield to find the different tips and take what we could from them. My son was born just before we moved onto the trailer park, into our very own trailer paid for out of the scrap we had collected. From then on my man took to my Romani way of life. He became a dab hand at wheeling and dealing and although he kept his day job we would work together in the evenings.

I was much happier on the trailer site, but I still found the days long and lonely. If Terry had a bigger car I would've hitched up the trailer and travelled. One day I heard the women on the park telling each other about a group of Gypsies who had pulled in up the lanes. Well,

Arthur Benham and myself at Stow-on-the-Wold Fair in the Eighties.

off I went to look for them, thinking I could at least welcome them and while away some of the day. I pushed me pram up and down the lanes until I spotted the trailers unhitched at the side of the road.

Oh, this was right up my street. I had other Travellers to visit – and, not only that, but it turned out to be Arthur and Renee Benham, a lovely couple who we had picked hops and peas alongside many a time in the past. They agreed to come by the park in the mornings so I could come along with me baby to drop rag-bills, but it was not to last. Soon the police moved them on and I was once again on my own.

Not long after this I found out that I was expecting to go to bed with a second child. I had my second son on the park and felt my family was complete. My days were now filled with caring for my boys.

One day, a man named Doctor Fox called in to see me, full of the joys of spring.

"Maggie," he said joyfully, "I have got some really good news for you and the other families on the park."

"What's that then, Doctor?" I asked him.

"A nice brand-new house! I've got you a brand-new house to move into."

"What is you talking about?" I asked, obviously upset. I didn't want no house! What was this crazy mush telling me?

"Aren't you pleased?" he asked, not understanding. "A nice new house."

"I ain't going in no house," I warned him.

"Oh but you are! They're not finished yet, but I've put your name forward for one and it's yours. I don't want to give it to anyone else."

"I shan't move into no house and that's that!" I said. I'd got to know Doctor Fox and liked him well enough, but he was not going to put me into no council house!

"Why don't I just show it to you?" he asked. "You'll soon change your mind. Let me show you the house..."

He kept on and on until I gave in, allowing him to drive me over to the half-built house. He was so pleased with himself, but I was not having it at all. He tried to soothe me as he saw the look on my face.

"It really is lovely, Maggie. Your boys will have their own rooms and there's a garden..."

"Doctor, I don't mean to upset you, but I ain't living in no house!"

"But the park is being closed!" he cried. "Your caravan will have to be moved. You must have somewhere to live. Now think about it, please!"

"When have I gotta move off?" I asked.

"A few months' time," he said. "You must've heard about it."

I had heard some of the women talking about it, it was true, but I had thought it was all talk. There had been no official word.

"If I go in that house, Doctor, I'll never be able to get out of it." I was sure of it. I knew that if I moved into a council house I would be there the rest of me life. Terry was a house-dweller, he would find it so easy to make it his home.

"Well, talk it over with your husband," he said.

"Over my dead body am I living in that place, so you give it to they that wants it."

I never slept a wink that night. My future looked bleak if I gave way to the doctor. No more green fields or lanes or hedges to look out on. I had missed it like a physical ache when we had lived in that flat. It was bad enough that I could not travel, as Terry had a full-time job, often working away from home for weeks at a time.

By morning I had a plan. If I had to live in a house, why not buy one that I could sell and leave when the time came? The next morning I took my two babies out on the bus and headed to the edge of Bristol that I knew. I got off the bus at Whitchurch to find an estate agents waiting for me opposite the bus stop. It was as if someone was guiding me.

Inside a man named Harry Hewer asked if he could help me.

"Yes, you can," I said, confident and certain. "I wants to buy a house where there are fields and trees and lanes to walk down."

Mr Hewer smiled. "I have just the thing."

He took me in his car and showed me a house not too far up the road. It was far from ideal, but I could see the open countryside out of the windows. I could walk to me heart's content up the lanes and roads.

"I'll have it," I said. We went back to his office for he had paperwork to fill in.

"Have you a deposit?" he asked.

"No, I've no money."

"Have you a job?"

"No," I said. "But me man has."

"What does he earn? What are his wages?"

"I don't know," I said.

"Then you'd better find out and bring him to see me."

"I can't do that," I said, "he's hardly ever home."

Mr Hewer looked at me for a long minute. "You'd better tell me what's going on."

I sat and told him all my problems: that I was a Traveller and my site was closing down, that Dr Fox wanted to put me in a council house. Somehow this mush seemed to understand how I felt.

"Have you nothing you could sell to get the deposit?"

"I could sell me trailer," I said. It was the only thing I had of value.

"How much do you know about the villages round here?" he asked me.

"I have stopped around most of them," I said. "I know me way really well. Why?"

"Can you use a camera?"

"I could soon enough learn to," I said.

"Right, we're in business," he grinned.

So it was that not only did I buy the house but I had got me a job. I was to get the bus each day with me babies and a loaded camera and take photos of any houses that were for sale in the outlying villages of Bristol. I spoke to owners, too, explaining that Mr Hewer could sell their properties and giving them his contact details.

It took weeks to set up and when my Terry came home for the weekend I told him we were moving. He didn't put up much of a fight, though he probably would have if he'd known that I had signed his name on the paperwork!

After I sold me trailer I moved into the empty house. We didn't have a stick of furniture or a single carpet laid, just an old cooker that had been left in the house. Terry was still working away, but Mr Hewer paid me enough for my work that I was able to get a second-hand bed for the main room and beds for the boys. I didn't really need much else. The house was just to sleep in really, for each day I was out working or walking with my two boys for miles. Terry came back whenever he could and my family visited me often. I had it made but for one thing. Soon they started building new houses all around me. I didn't like it one bit and me dad upset me deeply when he called in one day.

"Have you heard the cuckoo?" he asked me and I came up short. The cuckoo was a good-luck charm for the coming year and it was important to us to hear it in the springtime.

"No, dad." I realised that I hadn't heard it. "There's nowhere for him to pitch except the chimney tops – and he won't sing on one of they."

"No, my gal, you're right there." I was missing the cuckoo's sweet call for the first time and oh, how it upset me! I had been in that house a year. It was time to move on.

The next day I went back down to see Mr Hewer to arrange a move as far from the new dwellings as possible. "I can't stick it," I cried. "They're smothering me, they just won't stop building."

"Come on, Maggie," he said. "What's upset you?"

"Lots of things! The people round here don't want to know me. Worst of all there's no cuckoo!"

"What on earth are you talking about?" he said.

"I gotta live where I can hear that old bird," I explained. "It's bad luck if I don't."

He laughed of course. The old mush didn't know what I was talking about until I explained it all properly.

He looked at me sympathetically and then said, "Maggie, do you know the village of Paulton?"

Did I know Paulton! "Only like the back of me hand," I said.

"I have some bungalows being built in the village. They're only half built and I'd have to sell your house first."

"Mr Hewer, I wants one of they bungalows."

"Right then," he said. "You shall have one."

I moved in with me sister Emily until that little bungalow of mine was finished. She lived at Clandown, about two miles up the road from Paulton. When I moved into the bungalow my Terry was still away

*From left to right, my son Michael, Holly's daughter Michelle, me, Holly with baby
Bonnie and my son Jason, taken two years before Holly died.*

working, but it didn't dampen my sheer happiness to walk in my beloved
lanes again. I was home once again. Me children started in the local
school, for although they lived and understood our Romani lifestyle, I was
determined as me mam had been to give my children the best of all worlds.

I could easily walk down to me granddad's grave and by now poor
uncle Jim was also lying in the cemetery. He had been my favourite
uncle, so I would spend hours down there, walking and sitting at each
headstone. Emily would often join me. She had two children – a boy
and a gal – and we spent most of our days together. We were within
walking distance of Peasedown St John, but me mam and dad had long
since moved on. They had sold Keel's Hill and bought a bit of land in
Ashcott near Bridgwater – very close to the Swine's Jump Road.

If only I'd had any sense back then. I could easily have sold the
bungalow and bought myself a bit of ground. Land was so cheap back
then but, like many Travellers, I was ignorant of my own ability to do
it. I didn't realise that, as a property owner, with my man's work and my
own little job, I was well up the ladder. I could've chosen however I

This mare helped me cope with my sister Holly's death.
I would ramble for days on end, bareback and no reins.

wanted to live my way of life, be it in a trailer or wagon once more, but I wasn't educated enough to know my own rights.

In 1976 we lost my sister, our Holly. She was only twenty-five years old when she died and married with three little gals. We traced her illness back to our real granny, Minnie Black-Small. Every old woman who still remembered me granny had said how she used to swell up and be sick, lying in the bender tent for days on end, unable to get up and look after her little 'uns. Neither the local doctor nor the man from Exeter hospital knew how to treat her, or even for what. Minnie had died aged twenty-six, just a year older than our Holly.

Holly had been such a fun-loving, happy gal. She had been married to one of the Cole boys, who we had picked peas with as young 'uns. She had loved her three children with all her being. None of us could cope with her death, not least me parents, who couldn't bear to have lost another one of their precious chicks.

Only a day later, me mam had a massive heart attack and was rushed to Taunton hospital. Me dad took an overdose of his tablets, wanting to end his pain. Holly had been so lovely and beautiful to look at and always ready to laugh – she would've laughed if her granny's arse had caught fire. A happy-go-lucky, old fashioned gal.

She left a great gap in all our lives. We buried her in Glastonbury cemetery, on the hill in the sunshine. It was decided that me parents would bring up the three little gals, so Terry and I moved down to be nearby them.

We helped whenever we could, but I believe it was those three young 'uns that kept me mam and dad going. By now, most of me dad's family were dead and me mam was growing ill with heart problems.

In 1985 we took another big blow. Alfie died aged forty-six, leaving six children behind him. How was life to carry on without Alfie? No parents should outlive their chicks and here were me mam and dad, burying their third baby in Peasedown St John. He had never left the village we had settled in all those years ago and his whole family were there.

I was lost without Alfie. Life could never be the same for me now that I had lost my protector, my brother. Alfie – that little mush – had been my best friend and the bane of my existence. How I missed him!

I began working with me dad collecting scrap iron. It was our Alfie who had taught me to use the cutting gear to slice the iron up into bits we could load onto the pickup truck. I did this with me dad for eighteen years, taking the place of the son he had lost. By the end, I could cut and load iron with the best of them and I found it easy to drive the trucks, as my Terry had bought me a cattle lorry years afore. It was a six-cylinder T.K. which I would drive to all the horse fairs. I would hire myself out to farmers and families with newly bought horses.

It was good to work with me dad, but often hard for a small, short-legged person like me. He often forgot that I was a woman with her

Me dad with grandaughter Bonnie at Pedwell Hill, 1992.

own man and family and swung between treating me like one of his workmen and his own little gal. We often fell out, but we grew very close and I loved every minute I spent with him, so it hurt all the more when we lost him in 1998.

By the end his health was going fast and he would often stay home while me and a local man collected his scrap and weighed it all in. His old face would light up when we brought back the few pounds we had earned. We would do anything to make him happy, but no matter how hard we worked or how happy we made him we could not give him back his health.

Near the end we packed up and took him to all the well-known stopping places from my youth, everywhere his heart desired. Every day I would fill the tank with fuel and ask him, "Where to today, then, dad?"

We covered many miles only to find that most of our old beloved stopping places were fenced off or blocked with stones or fences. This upset him badly, especially when I took him back to Chapel Plaister.

"What the bloody hell have they done to our common?" he asked me.

"Well, my dad, it looks like I shan't be able to drive you round it today." I had been hoping to drive the car all round the common and let him see the old spots where we had stopped over the years, as he could not walk very far, but like many places we had returned to in those days it was now out of bounds to us. He was devastated.

"Where do my lot stop now?" he asked me.

"I really don't know, dad. It must be hard for 'em nowadays."

For the next six months we travelled hundreds of miles, until finally he could no longer get into the car to head off each day. Soon came the day that he took to his bed and three days later he was gone.

We never knew his real age as he had never been registered as a baby, so there was no trace of his birth to be found, but we worked out he must've been about eighty-four. To me, though, he would always be forty-seven. That was the age he had always given if anyone ever asked, even when he had been much younger than that.

Me dad's death left me shattered. I never again collected any scrap iron or made the Christmas holly wreaths. With his death, the old way of life was gone.

Chapter Twenty-five

Romani Rights

FOR MANY YEARS me dad had owned a piece of ground just up the road from his place. It was a horse paddock where Storm, his old mare, had lived for twenty years. She was left to me, so I bought the land off me mam and had the mains water put on for old Storm, for without me dad's old Landrover I could no longer manage the dozen milk churns I had used to carry the daily water up to her.

As so often happens when a family member passes away, our family split at the seams. We all fell out with each other many times over and though it was sad it couldn't be helped. Me mam was left on her own and started drinking, though she had always hated that old lush. She would phone me at all hours of the night, drunk as anything, either crying or singing.

In the end she asked each of us children to buy her place and stay with her. Terry and I sold our house and moved into a trailer with her. Soon, though, she changed her mind about selling us the place and ordered me out, so we ended up on the transit site at Middlezoy, near Bridgwater.

This was my first taste of living on a government site. We were only allowed to stay for twenty-eight days and I was frit as anything about what might happen to us after. What were we to do once those twenty-eight days were up? Yes, we had money from the sale of the house, but I couldn't bear to go back to another brick-and-mortar house. I had done my time of settled living. It wasn't for me and I felt I had suffered enough over the years. My boys were grown up now and I could travel like we used to do, but when I asked other Romanies about stopping places, I was shocked to find there were none left.

I was told that you travelled at your own risk and the risk was forever being moved on, from pillar to post. I couldn't believe what they were telling me. I had thought those days were over, but everyone I spoke to confirmed that we 'Gypsies' were being treated like animals.

What was I meant to do? Stop being myself? Give up all my way of life to make the gorgie happy? Should I put myself back in a house somewhere and lose myself?

I went to the council and was told to look for my own land. Me and my Terry searched for ground up for sale and, as we'd been told, took what we'd found to the council before we bought it.

I identified a piece of ground at Westonzoyland. "No," we were told. "We will not give you planning on that."

I identified a plot of land at Greinton, with cowsheds and a host of other buildings on it. "No," I was told. "That land isn't suitable for a Gypsy site."

My time ran out at the transit site, but they gave us a few extra days to stop as I had nowhere else to pull my caravan. We found nothing else and so did the only thing I could think of. We pulled into me dad's old paddock.

I thought that all I would need to do was visit the council and explain where I was, put in a planning application, but the village people got there before me.

GYPSIES MOVE ON TO LAND AT ASHCOTT

The newspaper headline was humiliating, for these people had known of my family for more than twenty-five years. Me mam and dad had lived at Pedwell for all that time and each Christmas most of the village came to buy their trees, wreaths and mistletoe bunches from us. They bought and sold our scrap. Poor Holly's three little girls had all gone to the village school!

A few days later I noticed a police car driving up and down past my place. Back and forth it went, so eventually I stepped out onto the lane to wait for it. As it passed me by I waved the driver down.

"Have you lost something?" I asked. They answered no. "Then why are you driving up and down this lane?"

The policeman in the passenger seat was holding a clipboard with lots of writing on it, turning it away slightly as I made a show of looking at it. The driver told me that a load of Gypsies had moved onto my paddock and, ever since, the houses in Ashcott had been burgled. The culprits, aged ten to twelve, had been seen coming in by my gate.

"Is that what all that writing says, then?" I asked, pointing to the clipboard.

"Yes," he answered.

"Well, mister, I got news for you. I can read what it says and there are no burglaries mentioned on that bit of paper." I glared at the two men. "I will now phone my husband and he'll be visiting your police station with a formal complaint, because you two is harassing me!"

With that they left quickly enough. The two policemen never came back, but things just went from bad to worse. I went to the council, only to be told they would get me off my land at all costs. I was given a planning officer to deal with, a woman more sly and nasty than anyone I'd ever met.

Terry and I visited her in the public council office and as she greeted us she turned to my man in front of the crowd of waiting people to ask him loudly if he was a Traveller.

"I'm not," he answered her.

"But you married into *that*?" At that everyone stopped and looked at us, as if we were criminals.

"You hang on, missus," I said. "It's nothing to do with you who or why my man married. It's planning I'm here for, not marriage guidance!"

So now I knew right where I stood. This was going to be the battle of me life – and what I knew about planning wouldn't fill a snake's eye. I was as ignorant as a newborn babe, but I vowed that I would learn what I needed if it killed me.

"You are not staying on that land," she told me plainly.

"Surely I got rights!"

"Gypsies have no rights," she answered.

"Is that so?" I glared at her. The battle had begun.

I spent the next few weeks tracking down other Romanies living on their own land, always dreading that I would return to find that my trailer had been towed out by the council. I was getting threats by the week until finally I found a woman who told me of a lady living in Bristol who might be able to help.

I went to see the lady, Penny Smith was her name, but she was so overworked she could only give me a small amount of advice and a copy of the *Buckley v. UK*[28] case that had gone to Strasbourg. Penny told me to read it over and over again, saying that it would help me to help many others of my race. She also gave me the phone number of a solicitor in Bristol, Brian Cox.

Our Robert was waiting for me when I got home. I gave him the June Buckley case to read since I was too worked up to concentrate. An

---

28. *Buckley v. the United Kingdom* was a legal hearing taken to the European Court of Human Rights in February 1996, which concerned Mrs June Buckley's battle to be granted planning permission for land she had owned since 1988. This was the first occasion that a problem concerning the treatment and rights of 'Gypsies' had been referred to the ECHR.

hour later he came back, leaping over the gate rather than waiting to open it. He was hollering like a dinalow[29].

"We got rights, our Maggie!" he yelled. "We got rights!"

"What do you mean?" I asked. "The council woman told me I had no rights at all!"

"Well, you have to let me read this to you!" and off he went, reading the words of a government circular numbered 1/94, which instructed councils to encourage private site provision, helping Romanies to help ourselves and advising us how to develop their own sites where legal and possible. I couldn't make head nor tail of it, but Robert was bright and if he said we had rights then we surely must!

By the time I went to meet Mr Cox I was worried out of me mind. Terry and I had spent a lot of the house money making our bit of ground liveable and we were frit that we would not have a case at all, let alone win it.

At first, Mr Cox wasn't happy with our case, but because my Terry travelled to earn a living and therefore hadn't given up our nomadic way of life completely, Mr Cox decided that we had a chance. Now we had a solicitor on our side and, having lost our planning application at committee stage, Mr Cox lodged our appeal.

---

29. fool

Chapter Twenty-six

The 'Land Grab'[30]

IT WAS TO BE A LONG SIX MONTHS before our appeal hearing and the council was still not giving us any leeway. One day, a man from the village came down to visit us. He had a bucket full of collection money that the villagers had pulled together to try and buy us out. £30,000 for a silly bit of land! They must have wanted us gone real bad.

To me, however, this wasn't just any scrap of land. It had belonged to one Lenard Smith: win or lose, I was not giving it up to someone outside of my family.

"Thank you very much for your offer, but this land is not for sale," I said. "Take your money and give it back to whoever donated it. I want none of it."

The villagers made a petition and, despite knowing us for so many years, only Mr and Mrs Foxwell stood by us, sending the people away with a flea in the ear. There were plans drawn up for a proposed dual carriageway which would have had a big impact on our appeal, for it

---

30. How the newspapers usually refer to retrospective planning applications.

changed the status of the land and made objections to our site on the grounds of increased traffic use less likely. This was good news for us, but the council denied the proposal even though we had letters to prove it.

At last came the day of the appeal and, even though we had been through it with Mr Cox many times, I was shaking in me shoes. My planning officer had hired a young Indian girl as her legal person, who seemed quite friendly and stayed close by me. Like a divvy, I took no notice of her until they came to visit the site. Then I caught on. Speaking Indian languages meant that the young lady could understand some of my Romani speech and I had been gabbing away to my Terry all day. It didn't matter, I had nothing to hide, but I was amazed at how low they were prepared to stoop.

Mr Cox could not attend my site visit after the main appeal, so it was up to me to defend myself. When the highway was discussed I again mentioned that the planned carriageway would knock out most of the Highway Department's objections to our site, but again the councilman said that the dual carriageway was a myth. I remembered that Mr Foxwell's land was being taken for the road and so asked the planning inspector if he would walk with me to their house where we could look at the letter he had received from the Highways Department.

The inspector asked the councillor if there was any need to visit Mr Foxwell and he visibly blanched, caught out by his own lie.

"It is true," he said, confirming that they had been lying all along.

Months later I heard that I had been given full planning permission to live on my own land. I should have been overjoyed, but what I had been through had taken its toll. I had been degraded in public, in the press and in my local area, just for being born a Romani. It took a long time for me to get over it.

I realised I had been suffering from this kind of racial abuse all my life, without knowing it. As time went on I discovered more and more about how my people were being treated in this country. There were things that made my hair stand on me head.

Due to my background mixing with lots of Romanies and house-dwellers alike, Mr Cox asked me if I would be a witness at various appeals. I began to learn of other people's hardships, discovering how much things had changed since the wagon times, when I had travelled along the lanes. The police had always moved us on, but it seemed that they were doing everything they could these days to escort trailers over borders and into other counties, as far away as possible. I was told that some of the Travellers' vans and pickups would barely have time to let their engines cool, or the Travellers themselves take a moment for they and their children to spend a penny before the gavvers were there to move them on again.

I couldn't imagine what we could possibly have done to deserve such treatment. Surely we had paid our dues by now? In the 1950s the government threatened to take our children away if we refused to give up our nomadic way of life. We had lived in terrible fear that we would be taken from our parents, never to see them again, yet only a scant few years before our men, boys and horses had fought and died in the two World Wars.

The more I became involved in these appeals to build private sites, the more I felt like I was helping my people, in some small way, to keep our culture alive. I learned a great deal by attending Mr Cox's planning appeals. My attitude was hot back then and every so often Mr Cox had to make sure I wasn't taking things too personally. I still had a long way to go and lot to learn and I suppose now that I had a great chip on my shoulder.

Our Robert started up the Romani Gypsy Council UK in Somerset and suddenly we had a title to work under. I found myself travelling to other parts of the country, looking at pieces of land, finding out what different families were going through. Without a bona fide address it was hard to get medical treatment on the NHS and enrol children into schools.

This was new to me, for even back in the wagon times doctors would come out and visit a sick Traveller at their camp. Suddenly you needed an address and National Insurance number – near impossible if your birth hadn't been registered or you weren't in school records. Many of us just didn't exist on paper or forms.

Robert and I were dedicated to our work. Our very first solo planning application was for a family in Frome, Somerset. We were so nervous, but somehow we won that appeal. It was a huge step for us. Then Mendip District Council challenged the planning inspectors' decision and won the case back. We appealed, of course, and the case went on for ten long years until the family won their right to live on their own land.

We learned from our mistakes and I continued to work with Mr Cox, who by now was working for South West Law, Bristol. Our reputation grew and grew and we were winning most of our appeals. To other Travellers, my name became bigger than me body and me phone number was passed out along with it across the country. Families from different parts of the country would phone me to help them, asking me to drive many miles to look at the land they had bought or found and dutifully I would identify it, only to be told that the council would not give planning permission there. Months or years later, I would see that land again with a house built on it. It was soul-destroying to see that land was good for one race but not another.

Mr Cox and I had a few retrospective planning appeals and I began to notice that families who were already settled on a piece were more likely to be granted planning permission than those who hadn't started building yet. From then on, if I found a bit of ground that was in line with circular 1/94 I would advise the family to submit a retrospective planning application. Though very few were granted at committee stage, most were overturned on appeal.

Retrospective was the new way forward! The families would move onto a bit of land over a weekend and make it just about liveable as we waited for the appeal.

The appeals themselves were awful. Through Mr Cox I was learning more and more about the law but I still could not stand the degrading way my people had to bare their personal circumstances in public. Every little illness or money trouble, how big and tall their children were compared to house-dwellers the same age – it was all dragged out in court.

At one appeal, a young mother was suffering from cancer. The gathered villagers clapped and laughed when they heard about it. I was mortified for her, shaking like a leaf on a windy day beside me, having to endure all that hatred. It was an uphill fight all the way.

To be a Gypsy, in planning terms, we have to be nomadic and earn a part of our living in a nomadic way. As most field work is performed with machines nowadays, we began relying on the horse fairs for our cultural and legal nomadism, selling bits and bobs, catching up on gossip and getting to know one another again.

It was a strange time, not least because we had to revert back to calling ourselves 'Gypsies', a long-disliked name. Since the early Seventies, roughly from around the time of the first Glastonbury Festival, New Age Travellers had started roaming up and down the country and it seemed as though people could not tell the difference between our two groups, not least the newspapers.

I hated it at first. If you had called me dad a Gypsy he would've been more than insulted, for that was a name that the house-dwellers called us, among other things. It was an insult. Yet, here we were, standing up in front of a crowd and saying, "I am a Gypsy!"

I have got used to it now, but hopefully we have slowly managed to educate the press into understanding that there is a difference between the many ethnic groups that travel the country, each of them with different needs.

The New Age Travellers are the newest travelling people. Not grouped together because of ethnic or cultural traditions but because they have chosen to leave conventional housing. Mostly they live in tents, buses or even horse-drawn wagons and they have learned to survive the best way they can.

The second largest group of travelling people in the UK are the Irish Travellers. Many of their number like to travel continuously, although I have done planning applications for many who want a settled base from which to educate their children, or who are in dire need of medical help. I get on well with most of the families and understand their needs.

The largest group of Travellers are still the ethnic Romani Gypsies, the hunted and hated race. Years ago it seemed that we were the only travelling group, but now we are in competition for places to stop and ways to earn our living.

It seems so much of our way of life is over. Hops are now gathered by machine and peas are picked by foreign workers who will work for less money than us. That means two important types of stopping place forever lost to us. Most of all the common land has been fenced off or blocked, impossible to access for a picnic, let alone unhitch for a night.

Perhaps this has caused some of the strife in local communities – now that so many of our historical stopping places have been taken from us, there is an ever-growing need for dedicated sites inside the villages and towns. Still, no one wants a Gypsy or Traveller living near them.

Yet often when I have done planning for a site, the gross opposition from the local people has been withdrawn once the site has been established and the families become better known to the villagers and townspeople. It must be a shock to find we are not so bad or different after all!

Chapter Twenty-seven

Organising Change

UNTIL I STARTED on this planning lark I never dreamed that there were so many Romanies dwelling in houses. I was amazed to discover their experiences and their particular suffering. Most hide the fact that they are 'Gypsies' from their neighbours and even friends, for they know from bitter experience that they might be bullied or worse. Children are often the ones that suffer the most. Beaten up, called dirty names, spat on. I remembered my own school days and was shocked that it hadn't changed since then.

I am the first to hold up me hands and admit that we have criminals among us, but that is true of every race and ethnic group. Not all house-dwellers are fair, law-abiding people, after all. Fear of racial abuse for these families can cause as much damage as any other crime. Many people have told me how hard it is having to hide their identity, living on a knife-edge all the time. They dread visits from their own family just in case the neighbours figure it out! I know many who have suffered health problems, mental breakdowns and all kinds of other difficulties.

I know one such family in Somerset, where the violent abuse against them and their children has become so out of control that we are holding meetings with the local racial equality department, council Housing department and the Police to try and find some solution.

Our people are often forced into housing by the simple lack of sites and pitches available to us. It all stems back to the 1960s, when the sites were first built. The councils built sites of ten or twenty pitches and placed families there, charging them rent and tax and everything else. The problem was that these sites were built in awkward, often unhygienic places, to suit the gorgies, not the Romanies who were supposed to live on them.

Old rubbish tips were grassed over to create sites, old filled-up cemeteries were covered over with tarmac and declared fit for us to live on. It is so against our culture to sleep and eat and live above the dear dead people, but it was never considered that being forced to stop atop of graves would affect us all. The camps built on top of tips would release methane gas and were overrun with vermin. In time we outgrew the camps, which were never planned to take account of our growth, and we ended up back out on the highways where we would likely be harassed and moved on continuously.

The more I discovered about these camps the more determined I was to encourage other Travellers to set up clean, private sites. I stepped up my planning and encouraged more and more people to seek suitable land. Mr Cox was snowed in with planning applications, but he handled each one very well. I was at his office most days, submitting appeals and helping families in their legal meetings. I must have driven him bonkers, but he kept smiling through it all, doing the work of several men.

As our reputations grew, we started to come to the notice of other planning groups. One day I got a letter from a woman named Siobhan Spencer. I had not heard of her, but agreed to meet her all the same. At last I had found another Traveller woman dedicated to Gypsy planning. She had been involved for many more years than me and had an office up in Matlock, Derby. Oh, I was alone no longer!

I went up to see her and was so impressed with her office and the planning they were doing, but most importantly of all I learned that there were other groups just as active as we were. I was invited to go to London with them to their next national meeting. I was completely overwhelmed with joy to see all these people, fighting for our rights.

I met Joe and Bridie Jones, a married couple from Kent who ran many worthwhile activities, and that great trouper Lenny Smith from Hampshire, who had been working for many years on Traveller issues. I greatly admired Lenny. He had achieved so much in his lifetime that I soaked up his advice, always looking forward to the chance to meet with him. Sadly, Lenny passed away at the end of 2007, but his work goes on in his memory. I miss him very much indeed.

I met many other people who were active in gaining rights for Romanies, including sisters Kay and Rachel, Andrew Ryder, Tom Connors and Richard O'Neil. They all dedicate their lives and time in one way or another into making this a better world for us. How I admire them all.

The only mistake I made on that first visit to London was getting the train up there. I had never been to that big city before, but after the meeting all I had to do was get back to Victoria train station and board me train, easy as you like. Not so easy for Maggie, though.

It seemed like there were a thousand people and even more trains. Dinalow that I am, I waited and waited and ended up watching me own train leave without me! I was so out of me depth I just stood there and cried. I needed a minder to sort me out. Instead of getting home at ten, it was nearly three o'clock in the morning when I finally got back. I vowed I would never get on another train. Now I go up and down on the coach and know me run as good as any rabbit in his warren.

Soon, Siobhan invited me up to Derby to join Derbyshire Police's 'Pride not Prejudice' group. It was my first meeting with the police and

I was a bit uppity and nervous. Could I stomach being friendly with a gavver on a one-to-one basis? Chatting and laughing with them? I didn't think so, not after how they had treated us over the years. I knew that me dear old dad, had he still been alive, would not have agreed to me being here and even though he was long gone I was still influenced by his principles.

From what I was hearing at the meeting these policemen wanted us to trust and work with them. I couldn't see that happening. At the meeting were several Traveller groups and lots of police officers. My misgivings were confirmed when Siobhan discovered that her phone had been stolen while she had been talking to a seated group of police officers. Even when she announced it on the mike for all to hear, the mobile wasn't handed in. It strengthened my gut feeling never to trust the law. I imagined that they wanted to check out the numbers on that phone.

I was not very impressed by that first meeting, but against the odds I went to a few more and realised that I could speak and make my feelings clear. To my great surprise, this was exactly what the police had been hoping for, wanting to build bridges and work with Travellers like me.

They knew nothing about our culture, customs or traditional way of life and, although I would never fully trust them, I thought that maybe, if a few of them could learn more about us, we might be able to understand each other better. They had a lot of work ahead of them to undo the old inherited prejudices the police force has against us, some still believing that we are dirty or all of us thieves. It will take many more years before there can be any genuine trust between police and Romanies. For instance, I learned that stop-and-search records are kept on all ethnic groups apart from a scant few, including Romanies, so there is no record kept that might shed light on our guilt or innocence or victimisation. When I asked why this was, I was told it was very simple.

"There's no slot on the form to record you. It's up to the Home Office."

So often, Romanies are ripped from their lorries or cars and roughly searched. There is no polite request to step out of our vehicle like any other Joe Bloggs on the street. If there were better records kept, this kind of treatment would be quantified and, hopefully, like with other minority groups, it could begin to get better.

No doubt it will be a long slog for that day to come, but if we work together we might be able to drop the 'them against us' attitude on both sides.

One day, out of the blue, I got a phone call from a young professor by the name of Luke Clements. He had heard about my work and struggles and invited me to become a member of the Traveller Law Research Unit (TLRU), an advisory group based at Cardiff University. At a TLRU meeting at the House of Lords I met a wonderful gentleman called Lord Avebury, whose family portraits hung in the committee room where we met. He is such a great advocate for Gypsies and Travellers and a lovely, down-to-earth man. I felt so humble in his presence.

No one can imagine how I felt as I walked into the House of Lords for the first time. I was a mere Traveller gal, born and bred in a wagon on the road, walking in the footsteps of kings and queens. I was so grateful to Luke Clements for bringing me so far.

Over time I have been asked to join many different groups, such as the Council for Racial Equality and police diversity groups. I give talks in school, teach councils about Romani culture and needs, and attend conferences.

By 2006, the old government circular (1/94) was ignored by almost all councils and many people like me were putting in retrospective planning applications due to their needs, so it was decided to make a new circular. Members of groups like ours were asked to attend meetings in London, where the government's Gypsy and Traveller Unit was based. Our first meeting was held in John Prescott's press room and there I met the then Under-Secretary of State, Yvette Cooper.

We soon realised that the biggest problem the government had was the caravan count, which was nowhere near accurate. Some counties hadn't even completed one. The government didn't have even half a true picture of how many Travelling people there were in this country, let alone how many of them were in need. Besides, how could counting a caravan tell you if there were one or two or six people living inside it? Their information was way out and I told them so!

Yvette Cooper invited a few of us back to her Whitehall offices for more discussions – that was an eye opener! I'd never set eyes on anything like it. The offices were old-fashioned but grand.

We had many more meetings before the new circular came into force, but finally it did. Circular 1/2006. There would be no more retrospective planning applications for me – seeing as I had consulted on it beforehand, along with other Gypsy representatives, and it was supposed to do away with the need for such action. This new guidance gave councils no quarter and had to be abided by. The only things that worried me were that there was still a shortage of suitable, affordable land and that the opposition of local communities seemed to be stepping up all the time.

No one will ever want one of our sites near them. It is as if all our hard work and efforts to teach people about our culture has come to nothing, but now the government has said that sites will have to be built and so we Traveller groups will make the most of what we have achieved. We will continue striving to get these people off the roads and to safer places where they can gain access to education and medical help, leaving at times to seek work and attend the lively horse fairs that have become more important to our culture than ever.

Since the industrialisation of the picking season, the horse fairs had become a real highlight in our culture, giving us the chance to meet up with old friends and new, for gossip to be let slip and old grievances brought up, debts to be paid and deals to be brokered. New babies are passed around proudly and young ones make sheep eyes at each other with a wink and a nod.

The horse fairs can be colourful and lively, a true joy to behold. Each year at Appleby hundreds of horses are took to the fair – mares and foals, trotters who show off their paces up and down the highway, dressed up in fancy harnesses and traps. There are traditional coloured cobs that pull wagons of gold, red and green, painted more beautifully than ever, all on show to be admired and envied.

People come in convoys by the dozen, pulling up on the fields to spend a few weeks of sheer bliss, wheeling and dealing, with stalls selling just about everything you could think of. If you can name it, you can find it at Appleby, from harnesses to baby clothes, ribbons and hats, pots and pans. All day long, horses of all colours are taken down to the river to be washed and rinsed: piebalds and skewbalds, red and blue rowans, light and dark bays. Where it's deep they can swim. The atmosphere never fails to stun me.

Chapter Twenty-eight

The Work Goes On

I HAVE BEEN INVOLVED with planning as far away as Birmingham, Cambridge, Oxford and Cornwall, helping to get hundreds of children into schools by placing their families on private sites. The days are long gone since we could manage without knowing how to read or write. I saw me mam and dad struggle at times, but nowadays being illiterate means you can't even pass a driving test or fill in a prescription form. Even employers looking for part-time help want a full run-down of an applicant's education, so it is more important than ever to get our young ones into schools. And oh, how proud it makes you to have a child who can read and write!

On one of my sites I know two grown men who had been disappearing twice a week. No one on the site could make out what they were up to. Months later, we found out that they had been going to a private teacher to learn to read and write. They were very embarrassed when we found out, but proud of themselves for the progress they'd made. They wrote their names down for me and I felt a lump rise in me throat when I understood how important it was for them to sneak off and learn.

The others on the site pulled their legs over it, but showed so much interest in learning that I advised them all to speak the Gypsy Education woman who visited the site. By now I expect that most of the adults on that site can write their names and addresses. That would be something to brag about!

I also knew a wonderful old man who had lived on sites and on the road all his life. He was a spritely, happy old man until his family was forced into a dwelling house due to the lack of available pitches. He hated being closed up in bricks and mortar and died within three weeks.

I have often let families use my home as their postal address to receive letters from consultants, or to get appointments from hospitals. Many of them travel miles just to pick up a letter and have me read it to them. I have been a go-between for one Irish family, whose son was very ill in hospital. Unfortunately, there had been a falling out between the man's wife and his family and she had banned them from visiting him. But after I wrote to the hospital on their behalf, the problem was sorted out and the hospital took the situation into account.

People can be so cruel without even realising it, but there is a lighter side to my planning work as well. I once knew a Traveller man who had bought a piece of ground near Droitwich, Worcestershire, that he wanted me to take a look at to see if it would be suitable as a site under the new rules. He could not read the address to give to me and so gave me directions instead, telling me to leave the motorway and take so many lefts and rights. I would see a big tree on me right, he told me, with a road branching off to the left. My instincts took me right to the gate and I could not believe me eyes when I pulled in and saw him there, waiting for me.

Me poor mam, who had come with me, turned to him straight away. "Don't you have any sense in your head?" she asked him. "How'd you expect my gal to find you all these many miles without the name of a village?"

"Well, I must have gived her good directions," he said. "She's here, ain't she?"

Me mam had no answer to that one.

Sometimes the folks I speak to have me falling about laughing.

"Hello Maggie," they'll say to me. "You're looking very well today!"

"So you can see me down your phone, then?"

"Yes and you looks very well!"

I just crack up at that. "I could do with one of they phones of yours!"

I had one man phone me up from Leeds, asking if I was that same Maggie who does the planning. "I wondered if you could pop up and look at me ground," he said.

"Do you realise I live way down in Somerset?" I asked him.

"Yes, but get on the motorway and it'll only take you an hour."

"It would if I had a helicopter! I'll put you in touch with someone closer to you."

"But I wants you," he said.

"Well, you can't have me."

"I'll ask you once more, Maggie," he said to me. "Is you coming up?"

"No."

"I'll ask you one more time. Is you coming up?"

"No," I told him. "It's too far for me to drive."

"Well, you're no effing good then!"

I laughed at that. "You're quite right. I'm no effing good at all!"

It takes all sorts, I suppose, but some of them think I can get up and fly! That particular man never phoned me again, though I have had men offer to buy me dinner in exchange for helping with their planning.

"Do I look like I needs feeding up then?" I asked him.

"Yeah, Maggie, you could do with a bit of meat on you."

"Do I get a cup of tea with me dinner?"

"No," he grinned. "It'll be beer or nothing."

I got him his planning and me pint of beer with me dinner. It's not all doom and gloom and I get to laugh with many wonderful people in me work. Some have given me little gifts for my help and I treasure each of them. I have been given a pair of milk churns, a gold brooch, a potted conker tree, wagon wheels, a whisky decanter (from a man who must have thought I was a lush!), wooden clothes pegs and flowers and many other beautiful things. I was also given a harness and saddle by one couple, who wanted me to ride me old cob to keep fit in order to continue with me planning!

The first few times I obtained planning permission I would gleefully drive down to tell the families that their appeals had been won and to explain the conditions attached to their permissions. I don't do this any more, for you never know how they will take such news! I have been thrown about, squeezed until me ribs ached, punched hard in glee and shock. I have seen grown men cry like babies, for they never really think that they would have such luck as to be living on their own land.

They break down and cry. No more hassle from the police moving them on, or bailiffs enjoying the chance to belittle them for the sport of it. They can register with a doctor and dentist, have clean running water and their own lavatory and put their children into school.

There is no feeling like the peace that comes with having a base to live from, to have a gate of your own to shut at night. The settled community take this security for granted, having known no other way of living. This is right and proper, but for us to share that security is really something else. It's like catching up with the rest of the world.

I must admit that, in doing all this planning, my people have made me into a bigger, better person than I really am. They have built me up into someone I'm not, believing I can make miracles happen, when really I can only work with the planning policies if I can prove families' need to live on a particular piece of land. It's a question of finding out in advance what the situation is with sites and pitches for the local authority concerned. Then I have to visit the proposed site in order to work out whether or not it fits the bill in terms of the planning rules. I have to bring to the attention of the council any illness suffered by members of the group, backed up by letters from doctors and consultants – forget about privacy, it all has to go onto the application. Ill-health plus the need to provide children with an education and the lack of existing sites are the main reasons I get planning applications through. But then when Gypsy families get planning permission they have to live under a set of conditions imposed on them (I had one that had forty-eight conditions added to it) – no gorgie has to go through this to get a house. I ask myself sometimes, why us then?

Although I have had great success in my planning career, a lot of help has come from people like Mr Brian Cox, my dear friend and planning teacher. He is so dedicated to his job and understands our needs.

Ron Stainer of Bath was another grand man. He did so much planning for Travellers before passing away in 2007 and will be sorely missed by all. Ron sent many letters and made many phone calls to keep me in line and up to scratch through the years. At times he would lay it on the line if he disagreed with me and often put me back on track. He was good for me and we became firm friends over the years.

Andrew Ryder is another favourite of mine. He introduced me to some good people. He too really cares what happens to Gypsies and Travellers and works hard for us.

Jake Bowers, a relative of mine, is out there doing his bit as well. He works with Rokker Radio, a radio programme made by and for Travellers and Gypsies that has become popular and well-known among Travellers and non-Travellers alike. There is also a network of hardworking Gypsy Liaison Officers working in different parts of the country, like Phil Eaton of Cornwall and Paul Goltz of South Somerset, whose dedication and sheer hard work have made a real difference on planning issues.

Recently I recruited a young Romani gal, Sally Tucker-Woodbury, to help me with planning applications. Sally is great and very enthusiastic. She runs rings round me, but at last I have a good, solid workmate who – most importantly of all – believes in what we are doing: getting homes, education and doctors for our people. We have started up the Romani Gypsy Advisory Group for the South West Region which is really taking off. I often thank god for Sally. With so many Travellers needing planning permission, she is truly like a second brain. Our phones just don't stop ringing, so it's kushtie to have such a partner. It enables us to do double the planning applications and get through twice as much work.

There has been a big turnaround concerning Traveller issues and the hard work of groups and individuals alike has highlighted the needs and problems faced by the Romani and Travelling ethnic groups. The latest assessments of needs to be carried out by the councils showed a need for 4000 extra pitches for Travellers countrywide. I believe that even this number will be like a drop in the ocean, but at least it is a start. I foresee the problem will take many years to sort out, if it ever is, until we can live without fear of racial abuse or harassment for our culture.

In 2003, the lovely young son of the Delaney family lost his life when he was attacked for being a Traveller at the age of fifteen. This child's death has had a lasting effect on the Traveller community – we are told that we must get involved in our local communities and have tolerance and patience, but we must bear a thought for young Johnny Delaney and his shattered family. We must be able to protect our children and to do that I strongly believe that we must have small, private family sites where we can show communities that we live by the law, pay our bills and – most importantly of all – are human beings and deserve respect.

Many house-dwellers who protest against sites being built don't even realise that they are inciting racial hatred against Travellers and it can cost our lives! If only these people would stop and think about why we need these sites, there would be far less heartache in this world.

Yes, things are slowly changing for us and though it won't happen overnight many pair of eyes are focussed on the councils, fighting endlessly to ensure there is justice in the planning system. I myself shall be keeping my own wary yocks[31] on the councils as I continue with me planning work. I have been involved in so many cases over the years that I tend to forget some of them, till I see a face at a funeral or a fair and remember how I fought for them and think to myself, "Yes, I got to know you well."

---

31. eyes

Chapter Twenty-nine

Our Forgotten Years

I F I WAS TO BE TRUTHFUL about it, what I miss most from me wagon days is the cold, crispy fall of the year, the hedges sparkling with frost. I often think of those hard, snowy winters and me dad picking the best sheltered spot to pull his wagon on. The smell of the wood being cut up on the saw bench and the big fires he lit alongside to burn off the unwanted wood, smoke wafting in the cold air.

I remember when he would be repairing walls and we would take out bottles of hot, sweet tea to him and sit in the shelter of the walls, out of the wind, while he took a brief break. I loved the anticipation of waiting for the spring to come back around, when new plans would be made as to where we would travel and what work lay ahead of us. There were many long hours sat with the family round the outside fire, old tales being told, bringing tears and laughter.

I was always struck by the sight of the first snowdrop and wild daffies, the golden kingcups, primroses and cowslips. Every spring we would see field upon field of buttercups and gather up bunches of elderflowers to dry in the sun for the next winter's use. During the long,

long summers the wild dog-rose would be everywhere, or the red poppy that grew in the pea fields and gave us all headaches when we picked close to them. I miss the cold, early morning mist out on the hop gardens, the drips shaking off the vines as me dad pulled them down for us to pick off the hops.

Sometimes, I even miss the sight of a police mush in a temper, telling me dad in no uncertain terms to shift on, me mam beside them trying to calm me dad down before he got himself locked up. That scene played out so many times that it is burned deep in me memory.

Most of all, I miss being on the move, the rhythm of our horses' feet and the comfort of our wagon, or running alongside it with our little Jack Russell rabbiters. It was grand, being near a different village each day but always knowing the love of me mam and dad and the closeness of me brothers and sisters. Summer or winter, we would wake up on a morning and fall out of the wagon to sit beside a good, hot fire. That fire was the centre of our lives.

That's part of my hope for the families I get planning for. On private sites we can return to our traditions, for to have an outside fire to cook upon and sit round is forbidden on authorised council sites as a hazard. If you sing and dance on a council site you're likely to get your marching orders for making a noise; if you bring a horse back to the site you're causing a nuisance to others.

There are so many things that are restricted on those sites that impact upon our customs and beliefs, but we are just Gypsies after all. Who's to care about us? These customs matter a great deal to me and many others like me who fight for the rights of Romanies and other Travellers. The planning will go on and on, until I become too old to do it any longer, for the rights of my people are worth it and it gave me a new lease of life. Like the old song says: if I can help somebody with a word or a song, then my living will not be in vain.

Photo Album

Me mam, Defiance Small,
at sixteen years old.

My real granny, Minnie Black-Small, sit-
ting down holding baby Bobby. This is the
only known photo of her, taken in the
1920s out calling in Torquay with a friend
shortly before she died aged twenty-six.

Left to right, Polly Frankham, me dad making pegs, me mam frying Joe Gray, and
Bob Frankham also making pegs. The Mendips, Somerset, c. 1936.

*A Smalls wedding in the 1930s. Mam was a bridesmaid,
second from left in the front row.*

*Mam's step-family: Aunt Ellen's only son, Roy, Willie, Sophie, Phoebe holding
Carol, Jimmy and Little Jimmy. Taken up Golvers Hill, Kingsteignton, Newton Abbot.*

Mam's brother Petrol Bob, in uniform during the last War.

Me mam's cousin and her two children with me mam, aged fifteen, in 1935.

After a school hockey match in c.1958: I am in the second row, second from the left.

Cousin Emily holding Holly,
my sister Emily, me and little
Lennie and Margaret.

Me mam with Maralyn, at 22 Keel's Hill
in the mid-Fifties.

At Bridgwater Fair, late Fifties: me mam, with her sister-in-law Ellen and her three children.

At Britty Small's wedding: all me mam's stepbrothers and sisters with, among others, granddad Jimmy (in the hat).

Me aged sixteen while living at
22 Keel's Hill.

Me dad's nephew Pepper with his grandson.

Harry One Dog, Cherry and me dad at Priddy Horse Fair:
"Bid me fair, Harry, she's a kushti gry".

Our Alfie with a friend. Alfie was one of
the top racers on grass in the South West.

*Cock-eye Joe, Ellen with her son Billy, me mam, Lil and me in 1967
in Peasedown St John.*

*Sallyann Smith, me mam and Sallyann's mother in 2003. I met Sallyann's
family for the first time when I did the planning appeal for her site in Evesham.
They are long-lost relations of me dad.*

Postscripts

Culture, Customs and Traditions

Death

WE HAVE A CUSTOM called 'Sitting Up'. Whenever we get wind that one of our people is seriously ill, if we are sent for or simply hear about it, we will travel great distances to be with their family, offering support and showing our respect to the person who is ill. If the person is at their own home, we will continue to come and go, but if we become aware (and generally we do this by instinct) that the person is passing away, we tend to spend more time with the family.

When the person has died, then their family will not be left on their own night or day. This is known as 'sitting up'. There will be a rota of other families that take turns to sit up with the bereaved round the clock. Most older people will bring tea, sugar and milk with them, to help out with all the tea that is made continuously through the day and night, for the immediate family will not eat until after the funeral.

The funeral will be arranged according to another old custom. We take our time and plan every detail. If the family is out of their area, the funeral may have many miles to travel back to the family cemetery, so time for the travelling is taken into consideration. The needs of older people are also considered: will they be able to stand the long journey? Who will stay behind to care for the elderly and young ones not attending the funeral? The ground for the grave will be carefully picked out – not under a hedge, a sunny spot is preferred. Much thought is given to the grave itself to make sure that it is suitable.

All kinds of wreaths will be ordered to be made up in shapes that meant something special to the person while they were alive: perhaps a horse and wagon or a pickup and trailer (towing caravan), even pints of beer and dartboards if that was what a man liked. Always we have the Gates of Heaven made so that the gates are open. All the mourners will bring wreaths as we show our respects with flowers, and so pickups or lorries may need to be booked to carry them all.

More and more we are reverting back to the old days and using horse-drawn hearses or good old London trolleys pulled by coloured horses to carry our beloved dead to their resting places. Wherever possible we have walking funerals with all the mourners walking behind the hearse. Respect is also shown by the way we dress for the funeral: black with a show of white (a shirt or blouse).

Graves are kept up, beautiful headstones are put in place, and our graves are very rarely without mountains of flowers all year round. Graves are frequently visited.

Respect for our lost ones is one of our principles. We all have principles.

Are Romani Gypsies Clean?

Yes we are. Our culture tells us we must be clean – not that we need any telling. It's born and bred in us. Our victuals are kept separate from everything else, and always covered by a cloth, even inside cupboards. Cups, plates, dishes, pots and pans are washed twice, once after use and again before use. Washing-up bowls are kept separate and never used for anything else. Bowls used to soak tea-towels and pudding-cloths are treated in the same way, and we keep a special bowl for washing our hands and face. A wife can have up to six bowls each of which is only used for one purpose. It is considered dirty, and a sin, to mix the use of bowls. When it comes to cleaning, buckets and bowls are the top priority.

Tea-towels, tablecloths and pudding-cloths are never washed with clothes. If a woman was caught doing a mixed wash none of us would accept anything to eat or drink off them again. They would be considered dirty. Mobile homes and trailers are kept spotless. We love pretty bedding and will often buy beautiful bedding at our traditional horse fairs: half of it never gets used as it's just for show.

Traditional Gypsy Horse Fairs

How we love to go to the fair. We will travel many miles to a fair, hundreds of miles sometimes, if we have to. There is very little that cannot be bought at the fair: gold earrings and chains, Crown Derby, Waterford glass, all manner of fancy clothes, shoes and handbags, everything for babies – even teats and bottles – mink hairbands and coats. You can get horses, harnesses, trolleys, carts, lorries, pickups, chickens, dogs, rugs and carpets.

And how we dress up! This is the time to show how we can dress and wear high-heeled shoes. While the women and gals strut their stuff, the men will be wheeling and dealing, earning a few shillings.

Can Gypsies Tell Fortunes?

Yes, some of us really can, so please don't underestimate the Romani Gypsy. It's not every Gypsy that can tell you your past or future. It's the ones whose families have stayed true to the old Gypsy blood, or as near as damn it. True Romani Gypsies are mystic – my mother and brother were very mystic. My mother could tell you things concerning the future; she could always tell if a woman was pregnant, even if only by a few days. When someone was very ill she could predict how long they had before they died and she was never wrong.

My brother Alfie could not tell fortunes but he could tell you where someone had died, such as in a house or a particular spot on a lane, especially if they had died a violent death. He could see spirits but could not talk to them.

As for me, I can't tell fortunes – and I don't believe in them. I prefer to let life come and go as it is meant to. I don't want to know my future or my fortune. But there are those of my race that could tell you yours if you wanted them to.

Romani Cooking

BELOW YOU WILL FIND a few of my favourite recipes. These meals were nearly always made over an open fire, using a kettle iron to balance the big black pots we had. When I was young we never had scales to weigh our flour or fat on. Instead, we would manage with a spoon or teacup and so developed a keen feel for the amounts that each recipe needed. Because of this, I can't give exact measurements for any of these recipes, but have included them to give an idea of how we lived and the sort of food we ate. Please treat these recipes in that spirit.

Roasted Meat Dishes

Christmas Dinner

Having got your man to get a kushtie yog[32] going with bundles of holly sticks or whatever he could lay hands on, get the good old black pots hanging ready on the kettle iron. Lay an enamel plate upside down in the pot.

---

32. outside fire

* Pluck and draw the goose before washing and drying it.
* When prepared, stuff the goose with chopped onions and a bit of sage, if you have it, before covering in salt and plenty of pepper.
* Lay the stuffed goose in the pot on the enamel plate. This saves the bird from drowning in its fat.
* Wash and peel plenty of tatters and onions. Part-boil the tatters with a pinch of salt. Put all the tatters and onions in with the goose, seasoned with plenty of pepper.
* Replace the lid of the pot and leave to roast for a few hours, until cooked.
* Put some water in a pot and bring to the boil over the fire. When the roast is almost done, add swedes and some chopped carrots to the pot.
* Season with salt and boil gently for ten minutes or to taste.

Hedgehog

We must not forget the jog-jog. Hedgehogs are eaten in the wintertime, as they are considered unclean in the breeding season, like most animals. To ready the hedgehog:

* Open the jog and wash it clean.
* Singe off the bristles over the fire.
* Push two thin stakes into each end of the meat to hold it open and push the stakes in the ground, close to the hot embers of the fire.
* Roasted, the hedgehog has the flavour of pork.

Pot-boiled Meals

With all pot-boiled meals you will need to top up the pot with hot water from time to time, so always keep a filled kettle singing on the fire. Never top up a pot with cold water, as this will stun the puddings, stews or broths.

Rabbit Stew

Though any meat can be used to make a stew, rabbit is the most common that we used. To make it:

* Fill pots with water and hang on the kettle iron, bringing the water to the boil.
* Skin and chop a fresh-caught rabbit and wash the meat until it's clean.
* Peel plenty of onions, tatters, carrots, swedes and parsnips and chop into fair-sized chunks.
* Place everything together into the pot, adding salt and plenty of pepper to season.
* To thicken the stew, mix plain flour and water into a runny paste and add slowly.

Swimmers/Dough Boys

A stew without swimmers – soft doughy dumplings – is far from kushtie. To make them:

* Peel and cut up an onion into finely chopped pieces.
* Add suet, plain flour and a pinch of pepper and mix with water into a stiff dough. Break pieces off and roll into small balls.
* Once the stew is three-quarters cooked, add the dough balls. They will swim on the top of the stew and cook nice and fluffy, helping to thicken the stew as they cook.

Joe Gray

This is the most common hot meal we cooked, with a smell so rich you can tell it from a great distance. To make it:

* Half fill a swing-handled pan with water and place it over the kettle iron to simmer.
* Wash and chop up tatters, onions and other veg (like swede or carrot) and add to the pan, seasoning with salt and pepper.
* After ten or fifteen minutes, when the veg is half-cooked, slice off

thick slices of bacon from your side of meat and add to the pot. As the water steams off, the fat from the bacon will finish cooking the meal, creating its own gravy.

* Using a skimmer or fork, keep the meal turning until cooked, adding a drop more water if needed.

Broth

As with stew, any meat can be used to make a broth. We usually used pheasant, beef, canni[33] or shushi.

* Wash and peel your veg – tatters, swede, parsnip, turnip and onions.
* Roughly chop and add to a pot of boiling water, already seasoned.
* Add your meat, followed by pepper, pearl barley and lentils if desired.
* Let simmer until the meat is cooked.

Suet Meat Pudding

This is another common meal. To make it, place a big black pot over the kettle iron, filled with water and simmering away.

* Wash your meat and slice into fair-sized chunks.
* Chop your onions, swedes and tatters and season with salt and pepper.
* In a bowl, mix plain flour, suet and a pinch of pepper with a drop of water into a stiff dough.
* Break off a quarter of the dough and place aside.
* Line a pudding basin with the rest of the dough, patting it firmly to smoothly cover all of the basin.
* Put the meat and veg into the basin.
* Cover the top of the basin with the rest of the dough, making a lid.
* Tie the whole basin up in a muslin cloth and drop into the pot to boil.
* Leave to simmer for an hour and a half.

---

33. chicken

Sweet Puddings
Christmas Pudding

These puddings were made at least two weeks afore Christmas and put in the kettle box under the back of the wagon – away from hungry mouths and itchy fingers. Me mam always made spare puddings around Christmas time, for they were much sought after by me dad's brothers. Here is how she made them:

* Get a big pot of boiling water at the ready on the kettle iron. In an enamel mixing dish put:
* Two cups of plain flour
* Two cups of mixed dried fruit
* Half a cup of brown sugar
* A pinch of spice
* Two large tablespoons of black treacle,
* A drop of brandy, if you've got it
* A fair lump of lard

Mix together with a drop of water till it's a good stiff dough. Split the dough in half and place each half into a separate, ready-greased pudding basin. Tie a muslin pudding cloth around each basin and drop in the pot to simmer for about one and a half hours.

Apple Dumplings

* Fill a pot with water and leave to simmer on the kettle iron.
* Cut peeled apples in half and core.
* In a mixing bowl, bind plain flour, suet, sugar and water into a dough.
* Break off a piece of dough for each apple, patting it out into a flat circle.
* Place two apple halves in the centre of the dough and add mixed dried fruit.
* Cover the apple with the dough, making sure it is patted firm.
* Tie each dough-covered apple up into a muslin cloth and pop it in

the pot to boil.
* Will take less than an hour to cook.

Spotted Dick

Again the old black pot should be filled with water and simmering over the kettle iron.
* In a bowl, mix together plain flour, suet and mixed dried fruit, with a small pinch of sugar and spice if desired. Mix with water into a stiff dough.
* Spread out the muslin cloth.
* Roll or pat all the dough into a big, thick sausage and place in the centre of the muslin cloth and roll up.
* Tightly tie off each end of the sausage with boiled butcher string and drop into the pot of water.
* Leave to simmer for just over an hour.

Custard Rice

* Put the rice into a small black pot, cover with water and leave to simmer.
* When the rice is cooked leave to cool down. Do not strain off the stock.
* Mix custard powder, sugar and tinned milk together and add to the cooling rice.
* Place the mixture over the fire to simmer for a few minutes, stirring all the time.
* The custard will thicken the rice and then it is ready to eat.

Pancakes

These pancakes come from an old recipe and have been made in the same way for hundreds of years. We often ate them as snacks in cold weather, such as when we were working on the pea fields and hop gardens. Once cold they are kushtie sliced in half and spread with jam.

* Have a good swing-handled pan hanging over the yog, with a dollop of lard melting in it ready.
* Mix plain flour with lard and dried fruit. When well mixed, add water to bind into a dough.
* Break off a bit of dough and pat it in your hand until you get a round, inch-thick piece of dough, about the size of a small plate.
* Pop it in the hot pan, making sure it doesn't cook too fast, and flip the pancake when one side is cooked, to brown the cake on both sides
* Turn out onto a plate and sprinkle with brown sugar.

Traditional Romani Crafts

As WITH ALL CRAFTS, great care should be taken with sharp tools, and children should only try these with adult permission and supervision.

Wooden Chrysanthemums

The common elder is used to make these beautiful wooden flowers. Each elder stick is chosen for its thickness and is made into flowers within hours of being cut, while it is still fresh.

All the sticks are stripped of their outer skin and laid to dry off. The size of the flower head is decided and determines how far up the stick you start to shave the slivers: the higher up the stick you start, the bigger the flower head you get.

* Make a point at one end of the stick. This helps it marry onto the privet better at the end, to make a tidy finished flower.

* Starting about three inches from the pointed end and using a very sharp knife, shave paper-thin slivers down towards the pointed end. Turn the stick after each sliver is shaved, to keep the head even. Each sliver will curl, and eventually they will all curl in

together.

* When you have a good flower base, start to shorten the slivers to build up the centre of the flower. Shave right down to the pith at the centre of the stick. By now you should have a large, white, fluffy chrysanthemum.

* Now you can dye the flowers in your favourite colours. We use left-over coloured crêpe paper. Soak each colour in a bowl of hot water. Dip each head in the bowl, shake and leave to dry. If you don't have crêpe paper, coloured food dyes work really well.

* To finish the flower, pick evergreen privet, break off the top end and push that into the pith at the pointed end to marry the two together.

* If you stand them in regularly changed water the privet will stay fresh for months and even take root.

* Two things to remember: first, it takes a lot of practice to make the perfect chrysanthemum – our men have been doing it for generations. Second, never ever burn left-over elder as it's bad luck.

Clothes Pegs

Clothes pegs are made from the nut hazel wood, in the old Romani way.

You will need the following: a sharp peg-knife, bradawl (to make holes in tin), thin tin/metal (to bind the end of the pegs to stop them splitting), a molly block (used as a knee workbench), small nails, and a small hammer.

* Cut hazel sticks, making sure they are straight and all the same thickness, so that your pegs match.

* Strip the outer skin from each stick.

* Using an old peg as a measure, cut the sticks up into peg lengths. You can do this on a molly block which looks like a fat, round log with the bottom half shaved thinner to fit between the knees.

* To tin the pegs you need long marrow strips of tin/metal – we cut

up milk tins. Bind the tin round one end of the peg, about an inch from the end. It must go right round and overlap. Make a hole through the place where it overlaps with a bradawl and hammer a nail in. Break off the excess strip and do the same for all the pegs. The pegs must be bound to avoid splitting.

* Now comes the chipping of the peg to make the mouth. Push the blade of the knife into the unbound end, turn the knife while it's in the wood and chip a segment of wood out. Put the blade back in and chip out the bottom piece. Now the peg needs to be slightly pointed around the mouth end. This makes a tidy peg. So, shave downwards from the mouth end to round it off.

* Now you must train the pegs. Take a length of stripped hazel. Push the blade of the peg knife into one end and cut right down to the other end. A stick of hazel can be cut into four trainers. Push the pegs onto the trainer – it should hold around three dozen pegs. Lay them out to dry.

All you have to do now is go calling door to door to sell them.

Wax Roses

Wax roses are made from many colours of crêpe paper, candle wax, and wire or wool to tie the heads onto evergreen privet.

* Leave the crêpe paper as bought, without unfolding it. Cut across the width, cutting it into three or four sections of equal size.

* Unfold one of the cut pieces so that you have a long streamer. Fold this in three and cut into three equal pieces.

* Take one of these pieces and fold the ends together. Continue to fold in half until you have a half-inch block of folded paper.

* With scissors, clip off both corners at one end of the paper.

* Unfold the paper which now has one side with peaks.

* Now for the fun part. You will need a flat-edged knife. Lay the paper across your knee with the peaks at the top. Taking care, take the knife and lay it on the very tip of the peak, press down, and

slide the knife down your knee to the bottom of the peak. The peak will curl over the knife, making your first petal. Do this to each peak.

* Now take the end of the paper and, using your fingers, press out a bulge under each separate petal.

* Put the last two petals facing each other with their bulges on the outside, then just roll up the strip, gather the bottom half together and tie it off tight with wool or wire. You should now have an open rose.

* Waxing your rose. We save up all the ends of candles – which should be white ones. Very carefully, melt your candles in an old pot. Children should not do this part.

* Take the melted wax off the heat and carefully dip in the rose, allow the excess wax to drip back into the pot and then leave to dry. You will have a thin layer of wax on the rose head which hardens to give you a perfect wax rose.

Tip: the candle wax will have to be reheated when it starts to cool. Cool wax will ruin your flowers. This can be a dangerous craft as the wax can burn or even ignite, so great care must be taken. Do not attempt it if you feel there is any risk.

The finished flowers can be attached to evergreen privet using short lengths of thin wire. If you keep the privet in fresh water, it will stay fresh for months.

As ever, practice makes perfect.

Wagon Songs

Dᴜʀɪɴɢ ᴍʏ ᴡᴀɢᴏɴ ᴅᴀʏꜱ me mam and dad used to sing many songs to the clip-clop of the horses' feet down the old tober. One I loved to hear them sing was 'My Living Shall Not Be In Vain', though those old lyrics are lost to me now.

One I do remember was called 'The Landlady' and me dad and uncle Bobby – me mam's brother – would sing it often. How we used to laugh when we heard this song from outside the pub door.

The Landlady

I walked into the kitchema[34]
To buy me some ale
And did that landlady
Put her gaze on me.

---

34. pub; alehouse

Do I owe you any vonger[35]
For me baccy, beer or ale?
If I do, my fine landlady
You must take it from me ragged tail.

I don't owe you any vonger
For me baccy, beer or ale.
If I did my fine landlady
You wouldn't find it in my ragged tail.

Me mam knew a sad little song, which I remember her singing now and then:

There's a Little Green Lane

There's a little green lane leading over the hill
To a little old cottage by the sea
Where two eyes of blue comes shining through at me.

There's a little old lady with silvery hair
There's a few in mine I can see
Your two eyes of blue comes smiling through at me.

If ever I'm left in this world all alone
I'll wait for my call patiently.
Your two eyes may shine, as I gaze with mine,
For your two eyes of blue will come shining through at me.

---

35. money

Common Romani Words

I HAVE ALWAYS THOUGHT OF ROMANI as my first language and English as my second, though in our everyday speech we often use a mixture of both. I love meeting other Travellers so that we can talk in our own tongue. I have listed some of the most common words below – spellings vary from dialect to dialect.

alladged ashamed

alvin meal

bal hair

bar a pound (sterling)

baulo pig

bootie work

buddica shop

buddica divvus shopping day

callin' selling door to door

canni chicken

chamming talking up a horse's virtues

chave / chavvie child / children

chokkers shoes

chop sell / exchange

chor / chore steal

churi / chori knife

dik look

dikkadooey / dikka kie look at this

dikkamengro television (literally 'look-box')

dinalow fool

'dordi, dordi' a common saying, like 'oh dear'

drag car, also road

drienga doctor

drom road (see 'tober')

dukker to tell fortunes

effets lizards

frit frightened

gansey knitted jumper

gavver-mush policeman

gell to come / go

gin to know

gorgie / gadjé non-Romani person

gounner bag

grunt pig

gry horse (see also 'tit')

gudler sugar

gudlie noise

guvs / gubs fleas / lice

hatch / atch to stop / stay a while

hop dogs caterpillars of the Pale Tussock Moth

hotchi hedgehog (see also 'jog-jog')

jank shit

jattue m.o.n.ke.y. [bad luck to say or write this word]

jigger gate / door

jog-jog hedgehog (see also 'hotchi')

johnsnails snail on a wall

jukel / juckle dog

juvill woman

keréngro house-dweller

kitchema pub

kosht wood / stick

koshters pegs, clothespegs

kriss king

kushtie good, fine, alright

kushtie bok good luck

lelled locked up by the police / in jail

long-tail r.a.t. [bad luck to say or write this word]

lush beer or other drinks in the pub

mandi me / I

mas meat

miler donkey

moaker mule

morkin scarecrow

moured killed stone dead

the Muller (noun) the Devil

muller (verb) to die

mullered dead

mumper tramp, hedge-crawler

mung to beg

murro bread

mush man

nappy gry bad or untrustworthy horse

O doughtie Oh dear, what now?

panch stomach / guts

pannie water, also to urinate

peerdie non-Romani / broke / homeless

pesser   to pay

piece   owned plot of land

pirroes   feet

pobble   apple

pooker   speak / talk (see 'rokker')

pookerin-kosh, pukker-in-cosh   sign post

poove   field

popper   gun

posh   not quite right in the head

prastie   to run and hide

putch   to ask / beg

raddi   night

rakli   posh woman

rig   outfit / suit

rokker   speak / talk (see 'pooker')

ruk / rukker   tree

ruv   cry

scrammed   frozen

shant   no

shirrill   head

shok   cabbage

shushi   rabbit

skimmish   half-drunk / been down the pub

skit   insult

slang   a licence (eg driving licence)

sloppie   tea

snope   hit

sootti   sleep

staddi   hat

tan   place

tit   horse (see also 'gry')

tober   road (see 'drom')

tov   cigarette / fag

tricklie   dirty

trushnie   hawking basket

uddruss   bed

vardo   wagon

vonger   money

yock   eye

yog   outside fire

youro   egg

Have you read...?

Nomads Under the Westway
Irish Travellers, Gypsies and other traders
in west London
Christopher Griffin

As warden of the Westway site, social anthropologist Dr Christopher Griffin had
a rare opportunity to immerse himself in Traveller culture. A proponent of
humane, experiential ethnography, he observed and listened to the Gypsies at the
site as he carried out his duties as caretaker. Lasting friendships were established
which deepened his knowledge of Gypsy society.

This scholarly yet personal account combines social anthropology with his
direct experience as site warden of the Gypsy encampment under London's
Westway. Reflective and partly autobiographical, *Nomads under the Westway* is a
history of west London's Gypsies and Travellers set in a broader context of
immigration and race relations.

Themes include the idea of London's 'foreignness' to the author as the child of
Irish parents, and again when he returns from many years abroad; also the Irish
in England more generally; and how the 'wheeler-dealer' culture forms an
integral part of the metropolitan economy.

Ambitious in scope, the book undertakes both a long historical view (going as
far back as 1800) and a detailed survey of cultural practice amongst Travellers
and Gypsies today.

Christopher Griffin is a Lecturer in Sociology and Anthropology at Edith Cowan
University, Perth, Western Australia. Born in London to Irish parents, he gained his
doctorate in Social Anthropology at Sussex University and spent seven years in Fiji
at the University of the South Pacific. Between 1984 and 1987 he was warden of the
Westway permanent caravan site for Gypsies and Travellers in west London.

ISBN 978-1-902806-54-9
Paperback; 384pp
£14.99 / US$29.95

Smoke in the Lanes
Dominic Reeve

A classic account of the reality of life as a Gypsy in the 1950s when Travellers lived in horse-drawn wagons and stopped by the wayside in quiet country lanes, but were often driven to 'atch' besides main highways as so many of the old stopping places were fenced off or built upon. This book is full of stories of life on the road and descriptions of colourful characters living for the present despite constant harassment by police and suspicious landowners.

Illustrated by the author's wife, Beshlie.

ISBN 978-1-902806-24-2
Paperback; 312pp
£9.99 / US$19.95

Stopping Places
A Gypsy history of South London and Kent
Simon Evans

"I cannot recommend this book enough to anyone with an interest in Gypsy life and history. Wonderful photos. I was delighted to hear all the quotes … A true account of a lifestyle that was snatched from under our feet"
Mick Harrington, a Kent Traveller, *Travellers' Times*

The county of Kent, the 'Garden of England', was also the market garden for London. The regular round of seasonal work – picking hops, fruit-picking and gathering peas, beans and other crops – attracted families of Gypsies who returned to the same encampments and worked on the same farms from one generation to the next.

Stopping Places gives vivid first-hand accounts of the traditional life of these Gypsies, living in bender tents and horse-drawn wooden vardos, until the mechanisation of farming began to reduce the need for casual labour. At the same time, life on the road was becoming increasingly difficult because the traditional stopping places were disappearing. Eventually a whole way of life was swept away, often violently, and the Gypsies were forced to live 'on the verge' or on officially designated council camp sites. Increasingly, the ultimate fate of many Gypsies today is to make the traumatic transition from a nomadic lifestyle to enforced settlement in houses. The events in South East England recounted here, with over 170 stunning photographs, mirror the experience of Travellers across the UK.

Simon Evans produces radio for the BBC and in May 2004 won a Sony Award for his work on Romany Voices for BBC Radio Kent. He is also a writer, photographer and video-maker. He has a longstanding relationship with the Romany community in Kent and is involved with a number of innovative educational projects which aim to integrate Romany culture into the school curriculum.

ISBN 978-1-902806-30-3
Paperback; 176pp
£14.99 / US$29.95

Winter Time
Memoirs of a German Sinto who survived Auschwitz
Walter Winter (translated and annotated by Struan Robertson)

"One of the most unusual and moving war stories you'll ever read"
Daily Express

"This marvelous little book sets the record straight and is an absolute 'must read' for Romani and gorja alike. It is a book that the reader will find rather difficult to put down again until he has read it all"
Michael Veshengro Smith, International Romani Guild, *Travellers' Times*

In this book German Sinto Walter Winter relates his remarkable wartime experience. One of nine children, he was conscripted into the German navy only to be discharged on 'racial grounds'. In 1943, together with two siblings, he was deported to the 'Gypsy Camp' of Auschwitz-Birkenau. Over a year later, shortly before the extermination of the entire camp, he was deported to Ravensbrück and from there to Sachsenhausen concentration camp. Grotesquely, before the war was over he was reconscripted and forced to fight against the Red Army on the Russian front.

Walter Winter recounts his memories of Nazi persecution with extraordinary courage and compassion. He does not flinch from recounting the dreadful crimes he witnessed in the camps and the cruel deaths of so many. The fate of Germany's Sinti and Roma at the hands of the Nazis is still too little known and *Winter Time* makes an important contribution to righting that wrong. In this book, extensive notes throw valuable new light on the policy of the Third Reich and successive post-war governments towards the Sinti and Roma.

Walter Winter lives in Hamburg with his third wife. After the war he worked in the family circus and funfair and, although now retired, he is still to be found at the Hamburg fair almost daily.

ISBN 978-1-902806-38-9
Paperback; 192pp
£9.99 / US$19.95